IN THE INTEREST OF
THE GOVERNED

In the Interest of the Governed

A Study in Bentham's Philosophy of Utility and Law

BY

DAVID LYONS

CLARENDON PRESS · OXFORD

1973

Oxford University Press, Ely House, London W.1

GLASGOW   NEW YORK   TORONTO   MELBOURNE   WELLINGTON
CAPE TOWN   IBADAN   NAIROBI   DAR ES SALAAM   LUSAKA   ADDIS ABABA
DELHI   BOMBAY   CALCUTTA   MADRAS   KARACHI   LAHORE   DACCA
KUALA LUMPUR   SINGAPORE   HONG KONG   TOKYO

PRINTED IN GREAT BRITAIN BY
HAZELL WATSON AND VINEY LTD
AYLESBURY, BUCKS

FOR SANDY

PREFACE

THE essay that follows falls into two main parts. The first concerns Bentham's utilitarianism, the second his theory of law. One is primarily an interpretation of the famous work, *An Introduction to the Principles of Morals and Legislation*, the other seeks an understanding of that little-known study, *Of Laws in General*. These topics and books are very closely connected, and the examination of one naturally leads to the other. But the two parts of the present study are somewhat independent and may be judged on their separate merits.

I propose a new interpretation of Bentham's utilitarianism. It is argued, first, that Bentham is not a 'universalist', and this is relatively easy to show. It also appears, however, that Bentham has a *dual* standard, with community interest the criterion of right and wrong in public or political affairs and personal interest the proper standard for 'private ethics'. The evidence that leads to these conclusions also suggests, moreover, that Bentham has a still more basic principle, which could be glossed as the idea that government should serve the interests of those who are governed.

I also offer a new reading of his theory of law. In the first place, it now seems clear that Bentham does not embrace a simple 'imperative theory', the notion that laws are to be understood as a 'sovereign's' coercive commands. For he acknowledges basic types of law that are essentially permissive, and these cannot be coercive. In the second place, even those laws that he thinks of as a sovereign's commands are not held to be, in a strict conceptual sense, essentially coercive. And it is interesting to see how Bentham develops these ideas by constructing what must be one of the earliest systems of 'deontic logic'.

It appears that Bentham has been misinterpreted. Perhaps this is because all but his most devoted champions have underestimated his depth, his subtlety, and his originality. My main purpose will be achieved if some readers are now persuaded to *read* Bentham, carefully.

The new interpretation of Bentham's utilitarianism was originally meant to be refuted. Employed to stimulate a careful reading of his *Introduction* in a graduate seminar at Cornell University in the spring of 1970, the outlandish suggestion resisted refutation. Requiring further exposure, it was presented in a paper read to the Royal Institute of Philosophy in October, 1970.[1] The original argument has been revised and elaborated—partly in response to criticisms, but mainly, it has seemed, as the natural development of Bentham's own ideas.

The work on Bentham's theory of law reported on below had two main stimulations. H. L. A. Hart first directed my attention to the wealth of interesting material in *Of Laws in General*. And I thought it wise to see whether that book would confirm my impression of Bentham's conception of the law as a system of social control. I soon found myself enmeshed in the subtleties of that important but unfortunately little known work. My attempt to understand it resulted in a paper later published in the *Cornell Law Review*,[2] which is reproduced with minor changes as the second part of this essay.

The main work for this essay was done in 1970 and 1971, during most of which time my family resided happily in London. I am grateful to Cornell University for providing the sabbatical leave; to the Guggenheim Foundation for their generous financial support; and to University College, London—especially its Department of Philosophy—for their warm hospitality. Many colleagues in London and at Cornell gave helpful comments, reactions, and criticisms, which I often took months to appreciate; as a result, I am unable to give full credit where it is due, and I take this opportunity of expressing my thanks as best I can. I benefited greatly from comments and other assistance offered by the Bentham Committee at University College, and am especially indebted to Professors Hart and J. H. Burns for their help and encouragement. Many other

[1] 'Was Bentham a Utilitarian?', *Reason and Reality* (Macmillan, London, 1972), pp. 196–221.
[2] lvii (1972), 335–62.

individuals made our stay in London enjoyable as well as productive. P. G. Welch in London and Carole Seamon at Cornell turned scraps into a typescript. Three children provided a contrapuntal background. I am grateful to Sandy for orchestrating. But that is only the smallest part of a debt that goes immeasurably beyond mere obligations.

D.B.L.

Ithaca, New York
April 1972

CONTENTS

xii CONTENTS

ABBREVIATIONS AND REFERENCES

A few abbreviations are used for works frequently cited. Certain titles are often shortened in the text as follows:

Introduction for *An Introduction to the Principles of Morals and Legislation*

Laws   for *Of Laws in General*

Bowring   for *The Works of Jeremy Bentham*. Published under the superintendence of his literary executor, John Bowring. Edinburgh: Wm. Tait, 1838–43. Eleven volumes.

Shorter acronyms are used for identifying passages quoted or referred to in the text from these two works:

IPML for *An Introduction to the Principles of Morals and Legislation*

OLG for *Of Laws in General.*

Such notes are incorporated in the text and placed in round brackets.

As many editions of the *Introduction* are still in use (and several are still in print) and most are, for most purposes, quite usable, it seemed inadvisable to identify passages by reference to the pages of one particular edition. The most generally useful references would cite the textual divisions actually employed by Bentham, which are reproduced in almost all editions; this is the system adopted here. A similar style of reference is used for other works, including *Laws*.

Chapters are referred to by roman capitals, paragraphs (the smallest numbered sections of Bentham's texts) by arabic numerals, and chapter divisions by lower case roman numerals. Thus, '*OLG*, X, ii, 6' refers to *Of Laws in General*, chapter X, section ii, paragraph 6. Volumes in the Bowring edition of Bentham's *Works* are indicated by roman capitals and pages by arabic numerals. Thus, 'Bowring, II, 199' refers to *The Works of Jeremy Bentham*, volume II, page 199.

The texts referred to in the *Introduction* and *Laws* are always those in *The Collected Works of Jeremy Bentham*, General Editor, J. H. Burns (Athlone Press, London 1968–). In that new and definitive collection, the *Introduction* was edited by J. H.

Burns and H. L. A. Hart and published in 1970. This text is little changed from those found in many other editions. (But users of the Bowring edition should be warned that the text in volume I of that collection was expanded to accommodate two spurious 'chapters' inserted by the editors after chapter XII, thus changing the original chapters XIII–XVII into chapters XV–XIX, as well as several other minor additions. I shall always cite the original chapter numbers, as found in most other editions.) The new edition of *Laws* in the *Collected Works* was edited by H. L. A. Hart and published in 1970. This text is changed considerably from that of the only previous edition of the same work, published under the title *The Limits of Jurisprudence Defined*, edited by C. W. Everett (Columbia University Press, N.Y., 1945). One should consult Hart's Introduction to *Laws* for a discussion of the differences.

I am grateful to the Athlone Press of the University of London, as publishers, and to Professor J. H. Burns, as General Editor, of *The Collected Works of Jeremy Bentham* for permission to reprint extracts from the *Introduction* and *Laws*; and to the current publishers for permission to reprint extracts from Jeremy Bentham, *The Works of Jeremy Bentham*, Reproduced from the Edition of 1838–43, Published under the Superintendence of John Bowring (New York: Russell & Russell, 1962).

INTRODUCTION

I

THE NEED FOR RE-EXAMINATION

1. *Introduction*

THIS is an interpretive study of Bentham's thought. It concentrates on two of his fundamental doctrines—the principle of utility and his analysis of law. Because many of his views are closely tied together, a study of this kind inevitably ranges far beyond its origins, and so we shall consider, among other things, his beliefs about human selfishness and conflicts of interest, his theory of punishment, and his attitude towards legal coercion. But the present essay does not attempt to provide a comprehensive exposition of Bentham's doctrines. For reasons to be mentioned, that is not yet possible. What is possible now, and is in any case necessary first, is to gain an understanding of the nucleus of his philosophy. This essay represents work towards that goal.

Attitudes towards Bentham vary widely, and perhaps we should begin by asking whether this enterprise can be justified. The short answer is this. Two hundred years have passed since Bentham's impact on philosophy began. In that time intellectual fashions have changed and more illustrious thinkers have emerged, from Kant to Russell and Wittgenstein. Some of Bentham's views look absurdly quaint or naïve today. But in the area that he chiefly worked, no one, before or since, has made a greater contribution or undermined the importance of his ideas. On many questions of ethics and legal theory it remains useful and sometimes necessary to begin with Bentham. He, more than anyone else, developed utilitarianism as a general theory of evaluation; with characteristic consistency and single-mindedness he applied it extensively and systematically. He insisted on rigorous analytical methods in legal theory, and he revolutionized jurisprudence by carefully dis-

tinguishing what law is from what we would like it to be, while
concerning himself with both questions.

But this is not the usual view of Bentham. He often pro-
vokes intemperate reactions, and in the recent past these have
generally been unfavourable. His writings are used to illustrate simple-minded philosophical positions which can be
readily summarized and efficiently refuted. Sometimes his
personal quirks and passions, his political campaigns and
bitter frustrations are studied more closely than his actual
words. He is seen as a pale shadow of Hume; as the man who
forged the intellectual shackles from which the more elevated
humanist, John Stuart Mill, struggled desperately to break
free; as the proponent of evil doctrines; even as one who sought
to profit from human misery. In this climate of opinion, it is
not surprising that otherwise conscientious philosophers
should sometimes ignore the *substance* of his moral views and
label as 'Benthamic' those whose values merely have a similar
form, such as politicians with little concern for human welfare
but who, like Bentham, 'calculate the consequences' of their
actions.[1]

Mill himself was more temperate in his assessment. He
judged that Bentham was a great reformer in philosophy, although not a great philosopher. Bentham had a practical
mind, Mill said, and he was sensitive to legal abuse and intellectual error. He applied his peculiar 'method of detail', with
striking results: 'He found the philosophy of law a chaos, he
left it a science: he found the practice of the law an Augean
stable, he turned the river into it which is mining and sweeping away mound after mound of its rubbish.' But he was
neither deep nor highly original; his vision was narrow and he
could not learn from others; he had no subtlety of mind and
lacked the 'power of recondite analysis'.[2]

Is this judgement just? Mill's verdict is clearly not without
foundation, and it has gained credence because of some obvious
contrasts between the two men and their works. Mill was more

[1] See, e.g., Stuart Hampshire, 'Russell, Radicalism, and Reason', *The New York Review of Books* (8 October 1970), p. 4.
[2] 'Bentham', reprinted in *Essays on Ethics, Religion and Society*, ed. J. M. Robson (University of Toronto Press, 1969), pp. 80, 83, 100.

concerned with the foundations and defence of utility than with its applications; Bentham was the opposite. Mill could compromise utilitarianism when he thought it lacking; Bentham never would. And Bentham could not even be credited with the basic idea behind his theory, for the 'greatest happiness principle' was in the intellectual air of Bentham's youth (and then, of course, the underlying idea was not new); and applications to the law, most notably to problems of punishment, had already been begun.[3]

Bentham's stature in legal philosophy has been somewhat higher. But his most important writings on law have been less accessible than those of his successor, John Austin, who has tended to overshadow Bentham. Without the evidence of his actual words before us, it has naturally been assumed that Bentham's theory of law is cruder than the Imperative Theory later developed by Austin. And, as Bentham suffered doubly under the attack on utilitarianism that ravaged Mill's supposedly superior position, so the recent onslaughts on Austin's views must have shrunk Bentham's legal standing accordingly.

The pendulum has begun a new swing, however. For Bentham is still the outstanding proponent of utilitarianism, the most important of all ethical theories. And philosophical interest in such theories—which offer a standard for judging what is right and wrong, or good and bad, as opposed to an analysis of value concepts—has been revived. Philosophers have begun to look afresh at the classical theories of Bentham and Mill, once they have realized that more modern and sophisticated versions of utilitarianism have few advantages to weigh against a high cost in complexity and lack of intuitive appeal.

We have also begun to find *new* things in Bentham. A generation or so ago, C. K. Ogden showed us how Bentham's theory of linguistic 'fictions' anticipated much more recent philosophical theories.[4] H. L. A. Hart has reminded us of Bentham's many contributions, he has applied some of Bentham's ideas impressively to current problems, and he has time and again shown us the value—if not the necessity—of starting

---

[3] e g., by Beccaria in *Dei delitti e delle pene* (1764).
[4] *Bentham's Theory of Fictions* (1932).

with Bentham when examining punishment and responsibility.[5]

But Bentham's most important doctrines—measured by their place in his work as well as their general significance—have seemed perfectly clear to us; there has been little doubt that they are understood. This confidence is misplaced. We have not really understood Bentham's utilitarianism, for example. I do not mean that its merits and implications have been uncertain (although that is also true); I mean that the principle of utility itself has been misconstrued. His chief work on law has hardly been read at all, and it turns out to be far more original and subtle than we assumed. This is, at least, what I shall argue in this essay.

If I am right, our judgement of the man and his work is ill-founded. It does not follow that when Bentham has been better understood his relative standing in the history of philosophy will change appreciably. But it seems we ought to try again to understand what Bentham said. This sort of job needs redoing periodically, for interests change and so do philosophical ideas. Old objections to Bentham's views that once seemed decisive may seem feeble today. I shall illustrate this later, after first discussing how Bentham's style of work gave rise to misunderstandings.

This essay revolves, then, about two issues—Bentham's principle of utility and his conception of a law. I suggest some new ways of reading Bentham. The issues are complex, however, and the evidence equivocal, so I cannot claim conclusively to prove my interpretations. But I hope at least to show that there are issues here, and incidentally that philosophical profit can come from exploring them. One cannot read Bentham seriously without reflecting on the largest, most important problems in the philosophy of morality and law, and some general questions are discussed in the course of our interpretive explorations.

2. Bentham's Life and Work

There is another reason why this study could not hope to be definitive. It concentrates on only two books in a vast sea of writing that flowed from Bentham's hand: his most famous

[5] See Bibliography.

An Introduction to the Principles of Morals and Legislation,[6] and its outgrowth, the virtually unknown *Of Laws in General.*[7] This limitation is not hard to defend, however. These are Bentham's most important philosophical works, and they deserve study on their own. They contain his most complete discussion of the principle of utility and the nature of law. And there are other reasons, arising from Bentham's own history.

Bentham was born in London in 1748, and he died there in 1832. He provides a bridge between David Hume (1711–76, whose *Treatise on Human Nature* was published in 1739 and *Enquiry Concerning the Principles of Morals* in 1751) and John Stuart Mill (1806–73, whose essay on *Utilitarianism* first appeared in 1861).

Bentham was the first of seven children, of whom only he and Samuel, the youngest, survived. Jeremy's mother died when he was eleven, a year before he entered Queen's College, Oxford. His father, a prosperous attorney, had high but conventional hopes for his obviously gifted son. After his three years in Oxford, Jeremy moved to Lincoln's Inn to study law. He completed his studies there, and, when age permitted, he was admitted to the bar; but, much to his father's disappointment, he never became a practising lawyer. He had developed other interests while studying, which did however centre on the law. Chemistry was one of the exceptions; he performed experiments in his rooms and corresponded with Priestley about them; but this was not his main preoccupation. From the mid-1760s onwards, Bentham chiefly devoted himself to a variety of political and philosophical projects that seem to manifest and to be unified by a great, continuing passion for sweeping reform in every corner of the law.

His original contributions to philosophy may well have been greater than we, following Mill's judgement, have long assumed. These derive from his writings, both published and unpublished in his lifetime, which we shall turn to presently. It may nevertheless be admitted that Bentham's fame is chiefly based not so much on strictly creative work as on his relative standing in social and intellectual movements. One of these was the group with which he was most closely associated, as its

---

6 *Introduction* for short.
7 *Laws* for short.

spiritual if not active leader—the 'Philosophical Radicals',
'Utilitarians', or simply the 'Benthamites'. This influential
conglomeration of notable figures included James Mill, for
example; it created the *Westminster Review*; and it led to the
founding of the first secular branch of the University of London, University College. Many of the reforms sought by these
men were inspired or explicitly called for by Bentham.
Another 'movement', of a very different character, in which
Bentham was involved from his earliest manhood, was the one
working towards legal 'codification' and related reforms. A
third movement to which Bentham contributed prominently
worked for prison reform. Several of Bentham's middle years
were preoccupied with his unsuccessful struggle to have a
prison built along the lines developed in his *Panopticon*
papers. He argued on utilitarian grounds for private administration of such an institution, and he wanted the first prison to
be put under his personal direction. One jaundiced critic suggested recently that Bentham's only aim was personal profit;[8]
in any event, critics then as now had little faith in such a
scheme, however upright Bentham's own intentions. This pro-
longed episode caused Bentham great frustration and made
him bitter. It also preceded (if it did not stimulate) his turn
from conservatism to 'radicalism'.

Bentham was well known abroad for his reformist principles. (Some of his most influential works were first published
in French, and many were read widely on the Continent.) He
was made a citizen of the new French Republic; but his general
approval of the rationalistically oriented changes there was
also tempered by his impatience with what he regarded as silly
philosophizing and 'anarchical' implications of the Declaration of the Rights of Man. Bentham had indicated similar
reservations about the various American declarations, at the
end of his *Introduction*; but his much more extensive comments on the French statement were not published until long
after the relevant events. Such intellectual disputes did not
prevent his moving to the 'left', however, and he eventually
came to favour representative democracy as the only satisfac-

---

[8] Gertrude Himmelfarb, 'The Haunted House of Jeremy Bentham', reprinted in *Victorian Minds* (Knopf, N.Y., 1968), pp. 32–81.

tory guarantee that government would serve the interests of those who are governed.

Bentham continued writing, and to some extent agitating, until the very end of his long productive life. When he died, at eighty-four, he was at work on the monumental *Constitutional Code*. Many of the reforms he advocated were eventually effected at home, and his writings on law, philosophy, and social policy have been influential far beyond the borders of his England. The full history of this influence has yet to be written. But the history cannot be understood until Bentham's doctrines are, and that is our main concern here.

Bentham's early writings range from work towards a plan for a rationally defensible penal code to a biting critique of Blackstone's *Commentaries on the Law of England*. Although he had amassed a great deal of material on legal offences and punishments by that time, his first book was on Blackstone, and it was, as its title, *A Fragment on Government*, suggests, a part of his *Comment on the Commentaries*. The *Fragment* was published anonymously in 1776, and its merciless scrutiny of Blackstone caused something of a stir; but the full work from which it was extracted was not published until 1928, after being discovered among the mass of manuscripts he left. Bentham's second book, *A Defense of Usury* (1787), made him well known, at least as a powerful reasoner and a defender of *laissez faire* economic policies (a position he discarded as he turned towards radical politics). Bentham's third major work to be published was *An Introduction to the Principles of Morals and Legislation* (1789); this was also the last that he completed for publication himself, without the help of an editor or collaborator.

At this point we must look more closely at Bentham's general orientation and his style of writing. We have noted that he was always more concerned to apply his utilitarianism than to analyse or defend it. As Mill suggests, this seems a count against Bentham's depth as a philosopher; but we must be cautious in our judgements here. For Bentham did work out, in enormous quantities of detail, the theoretical as well as more practical implications of his theory. And his priorities might even be defended on the basis of his utilitarianism. Also, he had sufficient philosophical perception, imagination, and acuity to allow himself to be driven into and usefully to pursue increasingly 'pure' philosophical questions.

It does not take much speculation to suggest how Bentham's utilitarian orientation could demand primary concentration on law, politics, and government. For he conceived the law as a system of social control whose malleability and place in human life provide it with the greatest potential for producing positive good as well as the capacity for causing great harm. It is understandable therefore that law and politics should become the focus of his concerns, and that 'private ethics' should never capture much of his attention.

But he also saw, early and quite clearly, that we need to *understand* the law before we can effectively change it—before we can hope even to criticize it accurately. He therefore found himself driven again and again to break new philosophical ground regarding law, human action, and motivation, for example. And he found himself obliged to do battle with those (such as Blackstone) who declared the existence of 'natural law' or 'natural rights'—men with whom he otherwise had much in common—because they tended to submerge this vital and complex subject in clouds of confusion and wishful thinking.

The two books of chief interest to us represent this process of Bentham's being partly driven into philosophy. As we have already observed, Bentham's idea of utility and of applying it specifically to the law was not original; he himself credits many others for inspirations, including Beccaria, Hartley, Helvétius, Hume, Montesquieu, and Priestley. Bentham wished to define the standard more precisely and to apply it with consistency, thoroughness, and rigour, on the basis of a full fledged 'science' of human behaviour. He pronounced his commitment to utility in his early *Fragment*, but he did not explain or analyse it very thoroughly there. That job was reserved, in effect, for the *Introduction*.

An Introduction to the Principles of Morals and Legislation must strike most readers as very strange indeed. One is likely to have first contact with it in, say, philosophy lectures, where it may be treated, rather misleadingly, as if it was intended as a general introduction to the principles of moral philosophy. But very little of it would be recognized by a philosopher today as part of 'ethical theory'. (Perhaps as a consequence, some parts of the book, which are essential to understanding his utilitarianism at that time, seem rarely to be read.) This is not merely the result of changes in philosophical interests and styles from Bentham's time to our own. Most of the book concerns legislation rather than what Bentham calls 'private ethics' (which is the main concern of today's moral philosophers, by and large); some of it even deals with judicial practice. A very large proportion of the book discusses problems of legal punishment in fine detail; a full third consists of an elaborate classification of possible legal offences; and the final chapter seems to be devoted to distinctions between various branches of the law.

Some of this, at least, can readily be understood. The *Introduction* grew out of Bentham's early work on a penal code; it was originally conceived as a theoretical prelude to a code he was intending to propose. But the code itself was not ready by the time the *Introduction* was fairly well completed, and the 'introduction' had meanwhile become long and deep enough to be published on its own. Before it was actually published, Bentham's ideas about its role changed somewhat; but the book was always meant to introduce extensive writings on legislation.

Almost all of the *Introduction* was completed by 1780 and was printed in that year, when Bentham hit a snag, printing was halted, and publication was postponed. The immediate difficulty was the distinction between civil and penal law, which is supposed to be the focus of the *Introduction*'s final chapter. The chapter could not be completed; Bentham began to see the depth and the wide ranging importance of the underlying issues, which involved the related ideas of a complete *body* of laws, on the one hand, and a complete *single* law, on the other. He thereupon dived into the study 'of laws in general'—that is, of the *nature* of law, as distinct from principles for rationalizing and reforming legislation. By 1782 Bentham had completed a book-length study of the nature of law. And when, after several years, he was finally persuaded to publish the original book from which this new one had developed, he did not finish the final chapter as originally planned but instead added a long Concluding Note which summarized some of his new findings and a Preface explaining the delay and his plans for future publications. The *Introduction* was published in 1789; but its outgrowth was not published by Bentham. Like the full *Comment on the Commentaries*, it lay among his manuscripts until discovered in 1939. It was first published (in 1945) as *The Limits of Jurisprudence Defined*, and it has since been re-edited from the manuscripts and given the more suitable title *Of Laws in General* (1970). This book, Bentham's most philosophical study of law, is of course hardly known and therefore was not considered in most assessments of Bentham's philosophical contributions.

By the time the *Introduction* was published, Bentham had written much more than he had prepared for publication, and few of his books thereafter were fully finished by him. He enlisted others to construct books from some of his manuscripts. This style of work has made Bentham's thought somewhat elusive.

For example, after the *Introduction*, the books that made Bentham most famous during his lifetime were actually put together by Étienne Dumont, who worked chiefly from manuscripts that Bentham supplied. The books produced in this way include the *Traités de législation civile et pénale* (1802, which first appeared in English much later, translated back by third parties, as the *Theory of Legislation*) and the *Théorie des peines et des récompenses* (1811, which had a somewhat similar career, except that it was divided into the *Rationale of Reward* and the *Rationale of Punishment*). Bentham had other collaborators. James Mill, for example, worked on *A Table of the Springs of Action* (1817); John Stuart Mill edited the massive *Rationale of Judicial Evidence* (1827); and, after Bentham's death, John Bowring, his literary executor, produced the *Deontology* (1834). Many of the books published within Bentham's lifetime are therefore not entirely his own productions, and these must be used with care when attempting to determine his ideas, to interpret his writings, and, of course, to trace his philosophical development.

But the difficulties are multiplied when one is forced to rely on the contents of John Bowring's first edition of Bentham's

Works (1838–43),[9] which is the only place where some of them appear. Many of the 'essays' included there were never actually written by Bentham, and they result from a considerable exercise of what might be called editorial initiative. Long manuscripts were severely, perhaps misleadingly, shortened; essays were compounded from manuscript materials and sections of published works (which themselves may not have been completed by Bentham, and may have been published originally in Dumont's French). Masses of material in manuscript form was never used, and we now know that some of it included complete unpublished works (the *Comment on the Commentaries* and *Of Laws in General*). Some of Bentham's previously published writings were excluded too, including his attacks on organized religion.

A new edition of Bentham's *Collected Works*[10] is now being produced, but only five of its projected thirty-eight volumes have appeared so far (three of the five containing only correspondence), and the rest will undoubtedly take years to complete.

This explains why one could not now usefully try to cover a much wider ground than we shall look at here. The materials needed for a comprehensive study of Bentham's work and an assessment of his philosophy are not yet available. But the two books that we have selected as the focus of our study—the *Introduction* and *Laws*—are fully Bentham's own, and we now have definitive texts for them in the new edition of his *Collected Works*.[11]

3. The Coherence of Bentham's Doctrines: An Illustration

I shall conclude this introduction by illustrating my earlier claim that Bentham's views need periodic re-examination. An objection against the very coherence of Bentham's philosophical doctrines will be rebutted.

At the beginning of his *Introduction*, Bentham sketches his

[9] *The Works of Jeremy Bentham*, published under the superintendence of his literary executor, John Bowring, 11 vols. (Wm. Tait, Edinburgh, 1838–43), cited hereafter as Bowring.

[10] *The Collected Works of Jeremy Bentham*, ed. J. H. Burns (Athlone Press, London, 1968–).

[11] The former edited by J. H. Burns and H. L A. Hart, the latter by H. L. A. Hart; both published Athlone Press, London, 1970.

basic principle for morals and legislation and his theory of
human motivation in provocative terms—full, as he says, of
'metaphor and declamation'—which begin as follows:

> Nature has placed mankind under two sovereign masters, *pain*
> and *pleasure*. It is for them alone to point out what we ought to do,
> as well as to determine what we shall do. On the one hand the
> standard of right and wrong, on the other the chain of causes and
> effects, are fastened to their throne. (*IPML*, I, 1)[12]

In this paragraph, Bentham may be thought to undermine
his own position. For, whatever one may think of these two
doctrines taken separately (and they are often criticized), their
combination is likely to be condemned by a philosopher today.
Let us see why.

The principle of utility is generally understood to require
that each of us always serve 'the greatest happiness of the
greatest number'. And Bentham's theory of motivation is taken
as saying that we are all naturally and inescapably driven by
desire for pleasure and aversion to pain, so that our actions are
unavoidably self-centred or 'egoistic'. These two doctrines are
firmly linked to Bentham's name. Few associations are as
powerful in the history of philosophy. But (one may object), if
Bentham maintains that each person inevitably tries to serve
himself alone (even if it means sacrificing others), then he cannot consistently and intelligibly say that anyone *ought* to serve
the general happiness. For it cannot be the case that one ought
to do what one is unable to do. Bentham's view of human
nature implies that it is impossible for me to do things that his
principle of utility requires me to do, such as sacrifice my own
happiness for the sake of others. So Bentham violates the fundamental principle that *'ought implies can'*. At the very outset
of his most important philosophical book, therefore, Bentham
blunders into absurdity. And he makes matters even worse for
himself by suggesting that these incompatible doctrines have a
common source, in 'nature'![13]

On the assumption that Bentham held the views attributed

---

[12] i.e., *Introduction*, ch. I, par. 1.
[13] cf. John Plamenatz, *The English Utilitarians* (Blackwell, Oxford, 1952),
pp. 70–2.

to him (which we shall later deny), let us see how the objection might be answered.

We may note in passing that the putative principle that 'ought implies can' has been applied here, as usual, in a transposed form: If a person *cannot* do something, then it cannot be the case that he *ought* to do it. But how, exactly, are these 'cans' and 'cannots' to be understood? No general explanation and defence of the principle has ever successfully been given, and arguments supporting it usually rest on examples and analogies. From these one can infer that it covers two kinds of case most clearly. There are, first, cases in which one is simply unable to do something, because of, say, logical or physical impossibility. In such cases (for reasons I shall presently suggest) moral prescriptions do not apply, so we cannot correctly say of someone that he ought to do the thing in question. But this is not all. There are also cases of what we might call moral or prudential impossibility, in which the moral or personal costs of doing something are regarded as excessive, because of a far more pressing commitment or stronger obligation, for example, or because it is thought that doing what otherwise ought to be done would involve too great a personal sacrifice. In such cases, it is not that something simply cannot be done, but that there are overriding considerations that justify or excuse our acting otherwise. (Words like 'cannot' and 'impossible' are sometimes used in presenting such a plea.) Let us apply this to the objection.

Suppose I claim that everyone is incurably self-centred and that no one will ever sacrifice what he takes to be his own best interests. Does this claim imply that one *cannot* sacrifice what one takes to be his own best interests—in a sense which makes the principle that 'ought implies can' applicable? For the principle to apply, either moral or prudential impossibility must be understood, or strict impossibility. Take these in turn. For moral or prudential impossibility to be involved, one must be prepared to claim that *any* sacrifice is *too great* a sacrifice— that this is the sense in which one 'cannot' ever sacrifice what one takes to be one's own best interests. But Bentham is not committed to such a view. It is not a corollary of '*psychological egoism*' (the view that we *are* all self-centred); it is a corollary of so-called '*ethical* egoism' (the view that it is *right* or *rational* for one to be self-centred). And Bentham's utilitarianism does not commit him to such a claim either. His trouble is supposed to arise from combining an egoistic conception of human nature with a *non*-egoistic principle of conduct. The former implies that a sacrifice of personal interest would not willingly be borne; the latter implies that it could be justified; neither implies that it can never be justified. So this interpretation of 'ought implies can' leads to a dead end.

Is Bentham committed to the claim on the other interpretation—that it is strictly impossible for someone to do what he takes to be against his own best interests? At first sight, the suggestion seems absurd. Bentham as a psychological egoist is supposed to say that we are all selfishly *unwilling* to sacrifice our own best interests, but this would not commit him to saying that we are all *unable* to do so. But it is true that Bentham holds a related view. For he does believe that our motives and our consequent behaviour are strictly determined by unswerving causal laws—laws of human nature. On Bentham's view of man and motivation, it is as impossible for me to act without such predetermination as it is for me to jump over the moon; and it is impossible in at least as strong a sense. Man is part of the real, natural world, the only world there is, and the mental and volitional aspects of his life are as fully a part of that world as the purely physical aspect. If a law of physical nature determines 'cannots' that rule out 'oughts', then the laws of human nature must do so too.

This, of course, has nothing to do with Bentham's supposedly egoistic conception of man. It turns entirely on the claim that one who places human action within the web of cause and effect leaves no room for the kind of human freedom that is presupposed by moral principles. But now the charge itself becomes notoriously controversial. Many who would otherwise oppose his views about human motivation and utility would nevertheless ally themselves with Bentham here and hold that the moral appraisal of conduct is perfectly compatible with the causal determination of human action. The issue is disputable, but no one can claim in this connection that Bentham embraces patently absurd and indefensible views.

Bentham's defence could be more aggressive. Let us examine the alleged incompatibility more closely. It should be observed first that his supposed egoism is not itself at issue. We are not asking whether his theory of motivation is correct, but whether it is incompatible with his utilitarianism. And one cannot show that two doctrines are *incompatible* simply by showing that one is false, even if it be granted that the other is true.

One might begin by asking whether it is necessarily the case that there are occasions for self-sacrifice. The answer is clearly no: logic does not guarantee that the interests of different individuals happily harmonize, but neither does logic preclude that possibility. This means that the mere claim, that there are *occasions* for self-sacrifice in favour of the general interest, is itself contingent. It cannot be said, therefore, that Bentham is constrained to believe in the possibility of such conflicts, on the ground that it is knowable *a priori*. This is important, for neither utilitarianism nor psychological egoism imply that there are such conflicts of interest. And so Bentham is by no means committed to the view that there are any occasions for self-sacrifice in favour of the general interest. But there are then no grounds for saying that Bentham's position is inconsistent. For the alleged conflict between his two doctrines rests entirely on the supposition that interests do conflict—not that they *can* conceivably conflict, but that they actually *do*. And Bentham is not committed to saying this, so his alleged position is not inconsistent.

This can be shown as follows. Suppose that Bentham holds the two doctrines attributed to him but also believes that personal interest as a matter of fact *never* conflicts in the long run with the general interest. Such a belief may be regarded as excessively optimistic and even naïve, but it cannot be considered absurd in the sense that it is unintelligible or otherwise impossible to defend against *a priori* objections. (We might even grant that the belief is false, without affecting the present argument.) Now, he can hold this view consistently with utilitarianism and with psychological egoism, for they have no argument with it. But then he would be committed to saying that there are no real occasions for a conflict between egoistic inclinations and utilitarian requirements. (Actually, the belief that Bentham must have for the present point is not simply that there are no real conflicts of interest, but that there never seem to be any to an agent who must make a relevant decision.

But this qualification does not affect the present argument, and it can be ignored.) We have, then, the possibility of Bentham's subscribing to these three points: (1) that the general interest ought always to be served; (2) that everyone always tries to serve his own best interests; (3) that there never is (or never appears to be) a conflict between the interest of an agent and the general interest. It is hard to see how the combination of points (1), (2), and (3) is inconsistent. But if they are not inconsistent, how could (1) and (2) *alone* be inconsistent? One cannot *make* two beliefs consistent by adding a third. So (1) and (2) must be mutually compatible. They can only be regarded as incompatible *on the assumption that* interests conflict in the appropriate ways. But Bentham is not required to add this belief to his collection, and so he cannot be convicted of inconsistency simply on the basis of subscribing to (1) and (2).

And, as a matter of fact, Bentham seems to have assumed that the interests of different individuals naturally harmonize in the long run—at least at the beginning of his career (when he wrote the *Introduction*), and possibly for some time thereafter. I shall later show how the text of the *Introduction* manifests this assumption. This may come as a surprise—even a shock—to anyone who assumes that Bentham's theory of punishment, for example, presupposes conflicts of interest. But that is a misconception, as we shall see.

Let us now return to the claim that 'ought implies can' and redeem a promise made before. One of the real truths underlying this claim would seem to be that moral principles, when they are applied to the concrete behaviour of individuals, apply only to the alternatives that are actually open to a given person at a given time. In this regard, Bentham's principle of utility is just like any other principle of conduct that purports to appraise acts as right and wrong, as things that ought or ought not to be done. What such a principle requires of me or forbids me to do is relative to what I am actually able to do. If I could jump over the moon or travel backward through time and by so acting could produce more happiness than by any other line of conduct that is open to me, then the principle of utility would require such things of me. But only then. So long as I cannot do them, it will not require them of me. Such a principle cannot require of me any more than the best that I can possibly do. This is one clear way in which a 'cannot' rules out an 'ought' (and thus 'oughts' imply 'cans'). If I simply *cannot* do something, if it is not an action *open* to me, then moral considerations do not apply to it. It cannot *be* something that I ought to do or ought to refrain from doing—because there *is no* such line of conduct for me to take.

Let us apply this to the original objection. Suppose that Bentham's theory of human motivation implies that I cannot do something. Now, his principle of utility is agnostic about whether I can or cannot do it. So, if Bentham can be said to have any position at all on the matter, he must be committed to the view that his principle does *not* require such an act of me. If the claim that 'ought implies can' has any lesson for us here, it seems, ironically, to be that Bentham's theory of motivation cannot possibly conflict with his principle of utility! It makes no difference, once again, whether Bentham's theory of motivation is egoistic. If it is, then it implies that I cannot do what I take to be against my own best interests. But then Bentham is committed, not to the judgement that I ought to do such a thing, but rather to saying that no such judgement can be forthcoming. What I ought to do is relative to the lines of conduct that remain open. It can never be a line of conduct that has been closed. The objection therefore collapses at a very fundamental level.

The objection might be modified in the spirit of some weak interpretations of the claim that 'ought implies can'. It may be said that, given Bentham's view of human nature, his utilitarianism is pointless and misleading. For he says that we ought to promote the general happiness, but his egoistic conception of man means that we are capable of doing so only when we think that it conforms to our own best interests. And this means that the only acts that a principle of utility can require of us are acts that we will do *anyway*. This makes the principle pointless, and misleading if it seems to require any more.

Actually, even if Bentham had an egoistic conception of human nature, it would not follow that the only acts a principle of utility could require of us would be done anyway. For there can be cases in which the general happiness is at stake but personal interest is unaffected, and the principle of utility would then require one to serve the general happiness, which is not something we would do anyway. But it should also be observed that Bentham's enterprise is by no means pointless given his assumption that personal interest converges with the general interest and his conviction that we have serious misconceptions of our own best interests and how they can be served. Bentham was always clear that one of the main points of his work was to show what our true interests are, how they can be determined in dealing with specific political problems, and how action in conformity with them can be encouraged if not guaranteed. His work is also not misleading, therefore.

I have said enough, I think, to acquit Bentham of the charges against him. We can see how one type of argument designed to show the incoherence of Bentham's position cannot succeed, and how bias against Bentham based on such suspicions is entirely indefensible.

But I have also suggested something more radical—that Bentham's actual views were quite different from the ones generally attributed to him. He not only assumes that interests naturally harmonize; he also fails to embrace psychological egoism. I shall argue that Bentham allows for fundamental, irreducible non-egoistic motivation, and that his view of man as motivated by desire for pleasure and aversion to pain does not have egoistic implications. We have reason to believe, in fact, that for most of his life he did not even think that selfishness is generally predominant.

Most important (though somewhat less important for the present objection) it will be shown that Bentham did not embrace a 'greatest happiness principle' of the kind so generally attributed to him. This is the main contention of the present essay, and the theme of Topic One, which begins directly. Hereafter, my arguments will be concerned with determining Bentham's actual position, not with defending or attacking it (though occasionally an interpretation must be defended on philosophical grounds, as we shall see).

TOPIC ONE:
BENTHAM'S UTILITARIANISM

2

A DIFFERENTIAL INTERPRETATION

1. *A Sketch of Bentham's Principle*

THE principle of utility, Bentham says, is the foundation of his work on morals and legislation. This is so, and in a variety of ways. The criterion of utility shapes his attitudes and judgements in every area of life. No philosopher has embraced a doctrine more consistently; none has ever attempted to apply a theory as extensively or systematically as Bentham has done. His principle determines his attitudes towards legislation, the use of punishment and reward, legal reform and codification. Its repercussions are felt even where one might think that utility had little to say. His analysis of human action and motivation and his theory of law, for example, seem to be arrived at by one who self-consciously assumes the standpoint of a legislator committed to the standard of utility. Even in the 'purest' philosophical investigations, Bentham never adopts a morally neutral attitude. This seems no accident; it is the deliberate approach of a thoroughly committed utilitarian.

But what, exactly, does Bentham's principle say? In most respects the answers have seemed certain. Rarely have commentators expressed any doubts or indicated any evidence that might not harmonize with a certain view of that principle. For our purposes, the most important assumption makes it 'universalistic', requiring that the interests of all persons (perhaps all sentient creatures, including other animals) be taken into account, on an equal basis, when action is evaluated. But I shall argue that this generally accepted view is unsatisfactory, for it ignores what Bentham actually *says*. His principle is not 'universalistic'. The beneficence it requires extends only to the

borders of one's community. More precisely, Bentham embraces a dual standard, with community interest as the test
within the public or political sphere, while self-interest is to
rule in 'private' matters. But these standards are also conceived by him as resting on a more fundamental principle of
utility—one which says (very roughly speaking) that government should serve the interests of the governed.

This aspect of Bentham's utilitarianism is not the only one
that could profitably be explored, but is the one upon which
we shall concentrate. We shall therefore ignore difficulties that
may accrue to other features of his position unless they bear
upon the main interpretive issue before us—the relations between community interest and self-interest and his principle
of utility. This means that we shall take certain supposed elements of his position for granted, for we shall not examine
them in close detail. Some of the assumptions that we shall
make will be indicated by the following sketch of Bentham's
principle.

Bentham's principle of utility is a standard for appraising
actions—for determining which are right and which wrong,
what ought to be done and what ought not. The principle is
comprehensive, covering all acts, including 'measures of government' (IPML, I, 7). It is meant to be complete in that appeal to a supplementary principle is never required. Utility
is also the ultimate criterion; it presupposes no other. It is
therefore what some would call Bentham's 'first principle'. But
the principle of utility alone does not suffice to tell us which
specific acts are right or wrong. In order to discover that, one
must apply the principle, and then one must be willing to pre-
dict an action's consequences. For it is the *effects* that acts have
(or that they are likely to have), and nothing else, which determine what one should do. Acts are approved to the degree that
they seem likely to promote happiness in particular. This is,
roughly, what Bentham means by 'utility'.

The principle is supposed to have implications for the law
and political affairs, and these are clearly Bentham's main
concerns. But what has such a principle to say about the law?
How can a principle that applies to human action have anything at all to say about legal rules and institutions? This is a

theoretical question, affecting at least the formulation of the principle, about which utilitarians have had remarkably little to say. Bentham himself is not entirely clear about the answer (although he is clear about its covering the law), but he does suggest some possible answers. There are at least two different ways in which such a principle might be thought to apply to the law. It could be formulated so that it directly applies not only to acts as such but also to legal rules or other objects to be evaluated. As acts are to be judged by their effects on human happiness, so laws could be judged according to effects that are assignable to them. An alternative approach would be to limit direct applications of the principle to actions, and then take in law (and anything else that needs to be included) indirectly. For the making or changing of a law (or the playing a part in a legislative process) is conduct of a kind, and it can be judged on the basis of its own utility. These two ways of applying the standard of utility to the law are not equivalent, as can be seen from the fact that the most useful *legislative behaviour* does not necessarily yield what would otherwise be judged as the most useful *legal rules*. In applying the test of utility directly to the law itself, we neglect the costs and benefits of changing or maintaining the law. For many purposes, however, these differences can be ignored, and Bentham does so when he discusses legislation in most general terms, without taking into account the special circumstances of the legislators. But the differences between these two approaches will not affect the substance of our main argument.

When Bentham explains what he means by 'utility', one is struck by his failing to differentiate between benefit, advantage, pleasure, good, and happiness, on the one hand, or between mischief, pain, evil, and unhappiness on the other (*IPML*, I, 3). This appearance is partly superficial, but perhaps not entirely so. By defining happiness as 'enjoyment of pleasures, security from pains', he makes one such differentiation (*IPML*, VII, 1). And other items on the list might well be defined by him, in somewhat different ways, in terms of pain and pleasure, which seem to be the basic items. A special complication is introduced by his including good and evil in these lists, for this may seem to commit him to what G. E. Moore

later called 'the naturalistic fallacy'.[1] But it is not implausible
to understand Bentham not as defining good as pleasure and
evil as pain, but as expressing fundamental value judgements
(*IPML*, X, 10). At the same time, however, Bentham could be
charged with using the various terms too loosely. Because his
use of 'pleasure' and 'pain' is somewhat vague, his overall position is uncertain and sometimes seems inconstant. He seems to
vacillate between the idea that pleasure and pain are felt sensations and the idea that they are the necessary consequents of
getting or failing to get something that one wants or has
wanted. Now, it can be argued that 'want-satisfaction' and
'want-frustration' in the latter sense are *not necessarily* accompanied or followed by any particular type of sensation of pheno-
menological condition, and thus that these two ideas should not
be confused. But Bentham seems to confuse them (although he
may simply think that there *is* such a relation). His position is
therefore open to criticisms along these lines. But this is an
aspect of his views that will not concern us any further. We
shall be content to say that Bentham values happiness or
human welfare most highly. And thus we are entitled to say,
in accordance with the usual jargon, that he is an 'ethical
hedonist'.

Now, utilitarians like Bentham are often singled out for
valuing happiness so highly. But they are, in fact, far from
alone. Many moralists seem to value happiness as much. This
is shown, for example, by those who hold that happiness is
the only fit reward for the truly virtuous. Such a view can be
ascribed to Kant. He seems to say that everyone naturally, and
rationally, seeks happiness for himself. But Kant believes that
justice should apportion it, joining happiness with virtue and
keeping it from the company of moral vice. Happiness must be
earned, and any claim one has to it can be forfeited.[2]

Bentham would not agree. Each person should always get
the best treatment that is possible. It may sometimes be right
to make a person suffer, but that should always be regretted,
never welcomed. Even the claim that someone deliberately

1 *Principia Ethica*, ch. I, esp. pp. 17–19. But in view of Bentham's 'imperational' conception of moral and legal discourse, it does not seem as if he could
have been a 'naturalist' in Moore's special sense. See below, ch. 6.
2 See, e.g., *Foundations of the Metaphysics of Morals*, ch. I, pars. 1, 12.

causes unhappiness to others is *by itself* no justification for making him suffer. For pain is an evil, and punishment essentially involves pain, so its use must always be justified. The only justification possible is that greater pain can be prevented or that greater happiness can be purchased. The pain imposed by way of punishment always counts against imposing it; no type of pain or suffering may be discounted. Likewise, no pleasure may be discounted—not even the sadistic pleasure that one may secure by deliberately hurting another. This is Bentham's view, and it is entirely consistent with, even demanded by, a thoroughgoing utilitarianism. It is a view that few are brave enough—or, as Bentham might say, unprejudiced enough—to take. But it should be observed that Bentham makes some reassuring assumptions. He reasons, for example, that sadistic pleasures necessarily involve someone's pain, and then assumes (without justification) that the pains due to malevolence always far exceed the pleasures. This enables him to conclude that malevolent action could never be justified on the ground of its utility (by bringing more pleasure to the sadist, say, than pain to his victim). (See Bowring, I, 81, and *IPML*, Preface, note a; XIII, 2, note a.)

Whose happiness counts? Bentham will not allow us to neglect the interests of a man because he does wrong or has a malicious disposition. Does he mean, then, that it is always necessary (at least in principle) to considers everyone's interests? This might seem to follow, and its plausibility is enhanced by a few occasional comments, such as the suggestion that only the 'most extensive' benevolence coincides with the requirements of his principle (*IPML*, X, 36–7). He also seems to say that animals should receive the same consideration, for they too can suffer (*IPML*, XVII, 4, note b).

This suggests a universalistic utilitarianism—the kind embraced by J. S. Mill and most (if not all) other utilitarians after Bentham, and the one we are most familiar with today. We tend in fact to think of utilitarianism as essentially universalistic. No wonder, then, that the standard view of Bentham's principle has it say that each of us ought always to be aiming at the happiness of everyone. Whoever is likely to be affected by an action (or by its alternatives, since an action is to be compared with its alternatives) must be given due consideration.

One may want to qualify this requirement, however, on the ground that it can sometimes be impossible actually to promote or protect the happiness of everyone affected because the interests of some might conflict with the interests of others and these conflicts can be beyond our immediate control. For this reason, it is sometimes said that the most generally applicable formulation of the utilitarian criterion is 'the greatest happiness of the greatest number'. Bentham uses the phrase himself, for just such reasons, and it can be found in many of his writings. It may come as a surprise, however, to learn that the phrase never once occurs in the book where he elaborates his principle most fully, the *Introduction*. It does not occur there because it does not represent his views about conflicts of interest when he wrote that book. And any universalistic connotations that the phrase may have are also foreign to that work. Let us see why this is so.

2. *Bentham's Parochialism*

Let us begin by taking a timeless view of Bentham's works, considering them as a whole. This will suggest a second way of construing his principle of utility—a way that is far better supported by the evidence than the standard universalistic account. Bentham could be thought to have a (let us say) *parochial* principle, which requires not that everyone be taken into account, but only those within one's community. (We can speak either of the interest of the community or of its several members, for Bentham believes that these are the same; see *IPML*, I, 4.) I shall argue later that this interpretation would be mistaken, for it fails to account for very striking evidence. But that Bentham's view is (so to speak) more parochial than universalistic may be shown as follows.

If we consider the whole of Bentham's works, we find that in the majority of cases, when he gives a prominent statement of his standard he imposes the parochial restriction. When he states what end ought to be promoted he usually employs some 'greatest happiness' or 'greatest interest' formula, to which he sometimes adds 'of the greatest number'. But in the majority of all these cases combined, throughout his published works, Bentham explicitly limits the interests to be considered to those of the community in question.[3] Now, there is no other kind of evidence to suggest that Bentham vacillated between universalism and parochialism. It is therefore possible to regard the majority of cases, in which the parochial restriction is imposed, as fuller statements of the appropriate standard and the minority of cases, in which it is left out, as elliptical. After all, Bentham states his full position so often, at the start of so many of his works, that he may well assume it amply clear and not in need of complete elaboration every time. It should also be emphasized that this restriction is imposed throughout the *Introduction* (with a few crucial exceptions): in the first chapter, as we shall see, and in the first paragraphs of Chapters III, VII, XIII, and XVI—wherever occasion arises to state the appropriate general standard. This evidence makes it extremely difficult to regard Bentham as a universalist.

One might of course try to explain such evidence away. An argument like the following would be necessary. Since the restriction is sometimes added but sometimes omitted, perhaps Bentham adds it when (and only when) he thinks that the interests within the agent's community are the only ones that are likely to be affected by the actions under consideration. This would not explain why Bentham saw the need to impose such a qualification when he made general statements of principle; but some explanation is needed for a defence of the standard, universalistic account, this one seems as good as any, and it is perfectly intelligible. But I believe that there is not a shred of evidence to support it. If we look at the various works (cited in

3 I have found the following examples in prominent passages of works ascribed to Bentham (volumes and pages in the Bowring edn. are indicated in parentheses):

The parochial restriction is explicit in *An Essay on Political Tactics*, ch. I, sec. 2, par. 1 (II, 302); *Principles of International Law*, Essay I, par. 7 (II, 537); *A Manual of Political Economy*, ch. I, par. 2 (III, 33); *Pannomial Fragments*, ch. I, par. 2 (III, 211); *Codification Proposal*, full title (IV, 535); *Official Aptitude Maximised, Expense Minimised*, Paper I, Preface, par. 2 (V, 265); *Introductory View of the Rationale of Evidence*, ch. I, sec. 2, par. 3 (VI, 6); *Securities Against Misrule*, ch. I, sec. 2, par. 1 (VIII, 558); *Constitutional Code*, bk. I, Introduction (IX, 4–5).

The parochial restriction is omitted in *Principles of Judicial Procedure*, ch. I, par. 1 (II, 8); *The Rationale of Reward*; Preliminary Observations, par. 1 (II, 192); *Leading Principles of a Constitutional Code*. sec. 1, par. 1 (II, 269); *Letters to Count Toreno* (VIII, 491).

the notes), we shall find no relevant feature linking those in which the restriction is omitted that is absent when it is imposed, or vice versa. Someone who wishes to stand by the traditional, universalistic interpretation may find reassurance in a few isolated passages, such as Bentham's ambivalent suggestion that animals' interests should be taken into account, or the passage suggesting that utility demands the most extensive benevolence (which can be understood, in context, as expressing opposition only to that 'partial' kind of goodwill that does not extend to all the members of one's community and that therefore fails to harmonize with the parochial standard). But a defender of the universalistic interpretation must also ignore a mass of evidence (only some of which has yet been cited) and turn his back upon the question why Bentham saw fit to add the parochial restriction.

Why does Bentham limit the interests to be considered to those within the community? If one considered only the evidence that is most readily available, such as the evidence I have already cited, from the *Introduction* and elsewhere, one might reasonably conclude that the basic principle is simply parochial. Whatever Bentham's reasons might be, and whether or not the result is a defensible position, no other conclusion would seem possible.

And this is striking, for a parochial principle has potentially significant implications. The interests of a powerful nation might tragically conflict with the interests of mankind at large, and one committed to testing acts by the interests of the agent's community could therefore find himself endorsing conduct detrimental to the welfare of mankind as a whole. A parochial political philosophy would have frightening possibilities in the realm of international relations.

But I shall argue that parochialism neither exhausts the whole of Bentham's position nor represents a basic principle for him. Bentham also seems to have come to more palatable conclusions about international affairs than his political standard of community interest might lead us to expect.

To the extent that Bentham is a parochialist, it is a most important fact about his doctrines. But the evidence which leads us to entertain this possibility should also force us to look at his writings with a fresh eye. We must not assume that his utilitarianism is a simple prototype of the view that later philosophers have considered.

3. The 'Explicit and Determinate Account'

It is time to consider what Bentham actually says when he gives his most elaborate presentation of his principle of utility, in the *Introduction*:

> By the principle of utility is meant that principle which approves or disapproves of every action whatsoever, according to the tendency which it appears to have to augment or diminish the happiness of the party whose interest is in question: or, what is the same thing in other words, to promote or to oppose that happiness. (*IPML*, I, 2)[4]

But whose interest is 'in question'? If Bentham were a universalist he would mean everyone's—at least everyone who might be affected by an act or its alternatives. But Bentham does not say that. Nor does he say what a parochial principle would require—that the interest of the community, or the interests of its several members, must always be considered. And the reason seems to be that neither of these is what he means. For he continues his account by explaining what he means by 'utility' (which presumably tells us more about what he means by the *principle of* utility). His concern is to emphasize that he does not mean by 'utility' conduciveness to just any end whatever, regardless of its connections with human happiness. He means specifically what promotes the welfare of persons. And in making this point he does seem to tell us more about his principle:

> By utility is meant that property in any object, whereby it tends to produce benefit, advantage, pleasure, good, or happiness (all this in the present case comes to the same thing) or (what comes again to the same thing) to prevent the happening of mischief, pain, evil, or unhappiness to the party whose interest is considered: if that party be the community in general, then the happiness of the community: if a particular individual, then the happiness of that individual. (*IPML*, I, 3)

[4] In a note added to the second edition of the *Introduction* Bentham formulates it as 'that *principle* which states the greatest happiness of all those whose interest is in question, being the right and proper, and only right and proper and universally desirable, end of human action; of human action in every situation, and in particular in that of a functionary or set of functionaries exercising the powers of Government' (I, 1, note a).

This passage argues strongly against the universalistic interpretation, and the parochial account fares no better. For it
seems quite reasonable to suppose that 'the party whose interest is in question', to whom Bentham refers in one paragraph when he states his principle, is the same as 'the party
whose interest is considered', to whom he refers in the very
next paragraph when he elaborates his notion of utility. And
Bentham says that this party can be *either* the community (or,
in other words, for Bentham, its several members) *or* some
particular individual. So, the principle as given *never* seems to
require that everyone's interests be considered—which rules
out universalism; nor does it require that the interests of the
entire community *always* be considered—which means that
Bentham's principle is not simply parochial. The community
must be considered in some cases, but only a particular individual need be considered in the others.

It must be admitted that the universalistic and parochial
accounts are not conclusively defeated. Apart from other evidence that may encourage one or the other of them (evidence
we shall look into later), one might try to explain away the
apparent implications of this central and definitive passage.
As before, one could hypothesize that Bentham speaks in these
narrower terms when (but only when) he believes that in the
relevant cases only the smaller class of interests would be
affected. We have seen how such an argument might run, in
favour of the universalistic interpretation, in the face of Bentham's frequent parochialistic statements. On behalf of a parochial interpretation (which we can now assume is more plausible than the universalistic account), the argument would run
as follows. Bentham basically wants one to consider the interests of all the members of one's community, but he believes
that sometimes only the interests of a particular individual
can be affected by one's actions, and then of course one need
only consider the interests of that person. The trouble with
this suggestion is similar to before: no evidence can be found
to support it, and there would be no reason for Bentham to
qualify his most general statement of a parochial principle in
such a way.

In fact, we can say much more. The rationale such an argument gives for Bentham's formulation is radically different

from the one that Bentham himself seems to give. For he does indicate his reasons, though in a place where few, perhaps, have looked.

4. *The Division of Ethics*

Our question is why Bentham says that the interest of the community must be considered in some cases, while the interest of an individual is all that need be considered in the others. An answer can be found in the final chapter of the same book, the *Introduction*. We should note that the first section of this chapter marks a return to his discussion of morals and legislation at the most general level, which he had suspended some chapters earlier. Bentham devotes the first two chapters to explaining and defending his principle of utility and the next fourteen chapters chiefly to matters concerning its application, which requires his analysis of action and motivation, for example, and the development of guidelines for apportioning punishments to offences. In Chapter XVII Bentham returns to certain more general theoretical questions, for this was originally meant as a transition to the proposed penal code. He wishes first to explain 'the limits of the penal branch of jurisprudence', but he approaches this by discussing the 'Limits between private ethics and the art of legislation' (in XVII, i).

After an introductory paragraph, he proceeds by defining 'ethics' (which is done, as soon becomes clear, from a utilitarian point of view). What immediately interests us is his language, which is striking:

Ethics at large may be defined, the art of directing men's actions to the production of the greatest possible quantity of happiness, on the part of those whose interest is in view. (*IPML*, XVII, 2)

That sort of phrase again: 'whose interest is in view'. Bentham defines ethics in the same kind of terms he uses in his 'explicit and determinate account' of the principle of utility. As we might expect from a general discussion of ethics from a utilitarian point of view, it looks as if further light may be thrown on the principle of utility.

We should also observe that Bentham defines ethics in

terms of 'directing men's actions' towards a certain end—the maximum happiness 'of those whose interest is in view'. Who are these persons? We find out from his partition of ethics, which is done by reference to the person or persons whose actions are 'directed'. This seems important, for he neither defines nor divides ethics in terms of those whose interests are *affected*, as the traditional view would lead us to expect.

The main partition of ethics is presented as follows:

What then are the actions which it can be in a man's power to direct? They must be either his own actions, or those of other agents. Ethics, in as far as it is the art of directing a man's own actions, may be styled the *art of self-government*, or *private ethics*.

What other agents then are there, which at the same time that they are under the influence of man's direction, are susceptible of happiness? They are of two sorts: 1. Other human beings who are styled persons. 2. Other animals, which on account of their interests having been neglected by the insensibility of the ancient jurists, stand degraded into the class of *things*.[5] As to other human beings, the art of directing their actions to the above end [this means, apparently, towards their own happiness] is what we mean, or at least the only thing which, upon the principle of utility, we *ought* to mean, by the art of government: which, in as far as the measures it displays itself in are of a permanent nature, is generally distinguished by the name of *legislation*: as it is by that of *administration*, when they are of a temporary nature, determined by the occurrences of the day. (*IPML*, XVII, 3–4)

Thus, Bentham divides ethics into 'the art of self-government', or 'private ethics', on the one hand, and 'the art of government' (which, from its parts 'legislation' and 'administration', seems to be government in the ordinary, political sense), on the other. (As Bentham elsewhere suggests, we might balance this terminology by calling the latter 'public ethics'. See *IPML*, IV, 2, note a., and Bowring, I, 195.) Ethics—at least from a utilitarian standpoint—has a dual character. But so does utility itself (and, presumably, the principle of utility),

---

[5] Here Bentham appends a long note opposing cruelty to animals. This may suggest that the principle of utility requires that their interests be considered and thus that it is 'universalistic', comprehending all sentient beings. However, the point is made precisely where Bentham is regarding animals as 'agents', and this suggests that it can just as well be accommodated to the interpretation of his principle presented below.

for it concerns the happiness of either an individual or a community.

It seems reasonable to suppose that the respective parts of the two accounts correspond, and it is easy to reconstruct the most likely correspondence. We are virtually told that the art of government is the art of 'directing' persons towards their own happiness. And government (in the ordinary sense) may be thought to 'direct' all the members of a community. This correlates the public half of ethics with the kind of utility that concerns the happiness of the community—that is, of its several members. The other correlation is then obvious: it comes by identifying the 'particular individual' that the other kind of utility concerns as the self-directing or self-governing agent of private ethics. Under the art of government, or government according to the dictates of utility, the interests of the entire community (or all its members) are promoted. The principle of utility applies directly to the government as a whole, which can be regarded as doing the relevant 'directing', and which is called upon to serve the agents that are governed, by way of 'directing' them towards their own happiness. Under the art of self-government, however, only the interests of the single, *self*-directing agent who is concerned are to be promoted, by himself.

5. *A Preliminary Account of Bentham's Position*

We have now seen Bentham's most elaborate, 'explicit and determinate' account of the principle of utility and also his explicit and definitive discussion of ethics from a utilitarian point of view. Since both are found in the same early work, written entirely by Bentham himself, it is reasonable to assume that the discussion of ethics faithfully reflects Bentham's own current conception of his utilitarianism. This leads us to a tentative reconstruction of Bentham's basic utilitarian doctrines as follows (to be modified and developed later).

The basic principle of utility may be understood as saying, roughly, that one ought to promote the happiness of those under one's 'direction', that is, those subject to one's direction, influence, or control. All free or voluntary human action may be regarded as constituting the 'direction' of one or more human persons (either the agent himself, alone, or others as well), and the fundamental normative idea is that government should serve the interests of those being governed. We may call this a 'differential' principle because the range of relevant interests to be promoted is not fixed in the usual way; they are neither everyone's nor all those within the agent's community. The interests to be promoted are the interests of those being 'directed' rather than those who may be affected. The relevant interest for the purpose of applying the basic principle—the interest 'in question', 'to be considered', or 'in view'—the interest to be served—is always that of the person or persons who are under one's governance, whose behaviour is subject to one's direction, influence, or control.

Furthermore, Bentham seems to conceive of this basic principle as if it applied in only two contexts—public and private. Ethics is *private* when a man 'directs' his own behaviour and no one else is subject to his control. He decides what he himself shall do; he does not direct others. ('Private' does not mean that others are not *affected*, but that others are not under one's 'direction'.) The standard that accordingly applies (by application of the differential principle) is that of self-interest. Ethics is *public* in the context of government in the ordinary sense. Here, too, we may speak of behaviour being directed, influenced, or controlled, and it should be emphasized that government, for Bentham, is concerned not merely with determining what people ought to do, but also with controlling or at least influencing behaviour—with *getting* them to do it. The government as a whole (as personified for example in Bentham's 'legislator' or his 'sovereign') may be thought of as 'directing' all the members of the community.

All 'measures of government' must therefore serve the interests of the entire community, that is, the interests of all its members. Bentham accordingly embraces two distinct standards,[6] one for each branch of ethics. In political affairs the happiness of all members of the community should be served, while in private matters one should serve his own best interests.

I should emphasize that this is a preliminary account, which we shall want to qualify in Chapter 5. But the evidence for a

[6] I shall call these two derivative principles 'standards' and their conjunction 'the dual standard' simply to differentiate them from Bentham's basic principle.

reconstruction along such lines is much stronger than one might at first expect, given the widespread unquestioning acceptance of the universalistic interpretation. The evidence is not uniformly strong; parts of the account are determined by explicit textual evidence, while other parts result from an attempt to forge a coherent whole that fits the tenor of Bentham's thought as well as the texts. The initial evidence is extremely strong. That Bentham embraces a dual standard— at least in the *Introduction*—is made clear not just in the prominent passages which we have already examined but also by his summary at the end of that first section of Chapter XVII, where the definition and division of ethics have been given:

> To conclude this section, let us recapitulate and bring to a point the difference between private ethics, considered as an art or science, on the one hand, and that branch of jurisprudence which contains the art or science of legislation, on the other. Private ethics teaches how each man may dispose himself to pursue the course most conducive to his own happiness, by means of such motives as offer of themselves: the art of legislation (which may be considered as one branch of the science of jurisprudence) teaches how a multitude of men, composing a community, may be disposed to pursue that course which upon the whole is the most conducive to the happiness of the whole community, by means of motives to be applied by the legislator. (*IPML*, XVII, 20)

Evidence like this is not, of course, absolutely conclusive, but it weighs quite strongly in favour of the account proposed, and it cannot be ignored. (See also *IPML*, XVI, 46, and Bowring, X, 560.)

The differential interpretation also enables us to account for Bentham's parochial restriction. In accordance with my earlier suggestion, let us assume that he has a parochial standard not only in the majority of cases throughout his works, where he explicitly imposes it, but also in the fewer cases, when he does not state it. We shall suppose that, while his parochialism is generally explicit, it is otherwise implicit and always there. Then we can note an interesting fact. Whenever Bentham says or (as we are assuming) implies that his principle requires us to promote the happiness of the community, he is concerned with what he would classify as political or public issues. The topics with which he deals in those places vary widely, from the character of law, through government structure and legal codification, to legal punishments and rewards, judicial procedure and evidence, political economy and tactics. But each subject falls under the public application of his principle, the part that coincides with the art of government. The parochial restriction is therefore not only consistent with but even required by the sort of reconstruction I am proposing. For, when the subject is political, his principle is taken by him to require that the interests of everyone in the community be taken into account. And thus we see that Bentham's parochialism, while undeniable, is nevertheless neither basic nor his entire view. It is drawn from a principle that requires us to promote the interests of those under our governance, the same principle that is taken to yield a different standard in private matters. It should be added that, whenever Bentham formulates his general position in the *Introduction* (outside the passages that we have considered closely), it has the parochial qualification added, and in each case it is clear (except for one case, to be considered, where it is arguable) that he conceives his main concern to be with matters of legislation or other public affairs. There is considerable evidence, then, that Bentham employs the standard of community interest in the appropriate places. This is true throughout his works (if we regard the small number of cases in which the parochial restriction is omitted as elliptical) and particularly in the *Introduction* (where no such added conjectures are needed).

Although we have so far considered only a few passages very closely, the ones upon which the proposed reconstruction is based are all prominent, explicitly general, and claimed to be definitive by Bentham himself. It seems fair to conclude that these passages place very severe constraints upon any acceptable interpretation of Bentham's utilitarianism. One would want very powerful reasons for discounting their apparent import. We shall now consider a variety of difficulties facing the new interpretation. None of these seems to invalidate the conclusion that the foregoing is the most defensible account of Bentham's utilitarianism.

3
THE CONSISTENCY OF THE
DUAL STANDARD

1. *Non-Equivalent Principles*

BEFORE defending this interpretation of Bentham's utilitarianism on textual grounds, we must pause to answer a possible challenge to our ascribing the dual standard to him, on the ground that we thereby burden him with an incoherent and therefore untenable position. Other things being equal, such an interpretation should be avoided; if there is an alternative way of reading the text that avoids imputing an incoherent view to Bentham, that alternative should be taken. We shall consider two forms of such an objection, each employing a notion of moral 'inconsistency'. The point of this discussion is to give neither a positive argument for the dual standard itself nor one for my interpretation, but to eliminate misguided objections to both. It will help us to get a better understanding of Bentham's position, and it will also have some more general implications.

The first charge to be considered is that the dual standard is internally inconsistent because the two standards can conflict. The political half of the dual standard says that one who governs others should promote their happiness, while the private half says that one should promote his own happiness when 'directing' his own behaviour. But consider the case of a legislator. He may be said to 'direct' others by establishing restrictive rules for his community, which (according to the political standard) should serve the community as a whole. But in legislating, as in everything else that he does, a lawmaker is deciding what he himself shall do as well as directing others. He is deciding, for example, whether to vote for a certain piece of legislation, and this immediately concerns some behaviour of his as well as the direction, influence, or control of others. But in deciding what he himself shall do, in thus directing his own behaviour, he is told by the private standard to seek

his own happiness. Trouble now arises because these two ends
can be incompatible. The interests of different individuals do
not harmonize perfectly, so the interests of the lawmaker need
not converge with those of the community at large. Voting one
way on a bill might be best for the community as a whole while
voting the other way would be best for his longterm interests,
all things considered. So, an occasion can arise in which, if he
serves the community best, he does not serve himself as well
as he could by acting differently, and vice versa. The dual
standard would then prescribe incompatible courses of action
for him, and its prescriptions in such a case may well be considered inconsistent. In virtue of what he could do to serve the
community, the political half tells him that he ought to do one
thing, while the private half tells him that he ought to do
another thing, which is incompatible with the first, in order to
serve his own interests best. At the very minimum, it would be
impossible for him to live up to both of the standards, so his
subscribing to both may be regarded as irrational. To make
matters worse, it may be said that one half of the dual standard
judges one course of action right, and all alternatives wrong,
while the other half judges one of the alternatives right, and
the first act wrong. On this view, then, a single act seems
appraised as both right and wrong (or both right and not right),
and if this does not amount to a downright inconsistency, then
it is the closest one can get to inconsistency in moral matters.

I believe that on my interpretation Bentham can be ac-
quitted entirely of this charge of inconsistency. The point is
worth pursuing a bit because it will help to bring out some
important aspects of his position; it may also help us to understand better the relevant notion of 'inconsistency'.

The *dual* standard is charged in effect with *internal* inconsistency. This would seem to be a special form of the claim
that *two* principles are *mutually* inconsistent. The idea of
possible conflicts between moral principles has played an important role in moral philosophy, for example in arguments designed to show that someone must surrender a principle because
it conflicts with one that a critic takes for granted. This form of
argument has often been used by those who reject utilitarianism because it is supposed to conflict with, say, a putative principle of justice. The same idea would also be used to show that

a person who holds conflicting principles must discard or substantially modify at least one of them—that it would be irrational to refuse to do so, knowing of the conflict. The dual standard is, presumably, in a similar position; embracing it is like accepting a self-contradiction.

To ascribe the dual standard to Bentham may well seem like saying that he subscribes to two distinct, independent, and clashing principles; one would be the principe of so-called 'ethical egoism' (corresponding to the private standard), the other a parochial form of utilitarianism (the political standard). Now, it should first be observed that these two principles are not logically guaranteed to conflict in practice, and it is conceivable that they never will. Egoism would rarely (if ever) counsel crudely self-centred behaviour, for it is hardly ever (if ever) in one's longterm interests to step on others' toes indiscriminately. Also, a standard that requires one to consider others' interests as well as one's own does not say that one's own should be neglected. It is not implausible to suppose that, taking the long run into account, and considering all factors, the two standards would prescribe the same behaviour in many (if not all) areas of life and in many (if not all) circumstances. But this is beside the point of the objection we face, which is that the dual standard is *inherently* untenable. Such principles *can* conflict, and this counts conclusively against accepting both. Other things being equal, then, we should not impute such a view to Bentham.

In general, the sort of 'inconsistency' at issue in moral philosophy is a conflict between two principles which are not logically guaranteed either to conflict or to harmonize. We can imagine pairs of principles that could be called 'contradictory' in a stronger sense, for example where one says that the promotion of self-interest makes an act right and the other says that the promotion of self-interest does not make an act right, or makes it wrong. When principles that explicitly say such things are combined together, the result seems plainly incoherent. But this is not the sort of case we have before us, nor is it usually (if ever) the sort of case that philosophers worry about. We shall refer to such 'contradictory' combinations from time to time hereafter, for the sake of contrast, but they will not otherwise concern us.

The first point I wish to make—which may already be apparent—is that ordinarily 'conflicting' principles are not, or need not be, strictly *inconsistent* with each other. In saying this I am not assuming any special views about the logical nature of moral judgements and principles, views which would lead me to deny that they can enter into straightforward logical relations with one another. Someone might say that judgements or principles are neither true nor false and conclude that they cannot be strictly inconsistent; but this is not my point. Someone might deny that 'X is right' and 'X is wrong' (or not right) are strictly contradictories; but I am not assuming any such thing. I am willing for the present to grant any plausible premiss about the logical character of moral judgements and principles which is needed to make the strongest possible case for saying that conflicting principles are 'inconsistent'. My point is that, even granting these premisses, the charge of 'inconsistency' against the dual standard and comparable combinations may trade on a misconception of their logical relations. Such principles are simply *incapable* of generating logically inconsistent judgements or prescriptions of specific acts. More precisely, they can give rise to such judgements only if we assume the relevant contingent facts about the world—facts that are not implied by the principles themselves. For example, the idea that personal and community interests sometimes conflict is neither true *a priori* nor implied by the two parts of Bentham's dual standard. It is a substantive point that must be argued independently.

To call such principles 'inconsistent' can be misleading; to use this kind of language to characterize the relations between conflicting principles of conduct may illicitly trade upon the logical force of strict inconsistency proofs regarding ordinary statements. We may suggest that logic itself condemns our simultaneously subscribing to principles that can possibly conflict, and in particular that logic abhors a dual standard. We think in terms of the following model: statement S is shown to entail statement p, and statement S' is shown to entail statement p'; but p logically contradicts p', so we can conclude that S is inconsistent with S' and that at least one of them must be given up. In the special case of a self-contradictory statement, we prove that S alone entails both p and p' where p

contradicts p', and thus that S itself must be rejected. But these are not the proper models for us, for they assume that no further premisses are involved in the deductions. Conflicts between principles generally turn on factual assumptions. We cannot argue: principle P entails judgement j and principle P' entails judgement j', but j contradicts j', so P and P' are inconsistent. A better model would be this: *given* some factual premise F, we can derive j from P and j' from P'; but (we are assuming) j contradicts j'. What follows? Not that the pair of principles, P and P', is inconsistent, but only that the triplet, P and P' and F, is inconsistent. It may be irrational to accept this triplet, knowing it to be inconsistent, but that does not show that it is irrational to accept the combination of 'conflicting' principles, P and P'. I shall now expand on this a bit.

A principle of conduct can be construed as saying that one ought to do things if they are of a certain kind—if, as we might say, the lines of action possess a certain 'criterial property'. For example, the criterial property of ethical egoism is being a course of action that would promote a certain end, in the long run, at least as much as any alternative open to the agent could do, the end being the agent's happiness. The criterial property of a parochial utilitarianism can be defined in similar terms, except that the end would be the happiness of the several members of the agent's community. A given principle may be said to favour an act if the act possesses the relevant criterial property; it may be said to oppose an act if the act itself does not possess it but an alternative open to the agent does possess it. Acts may be identified in many ways, some of which entail the possession by the act of the criterial property (for example, 'keeping one's promise' in relation to a principle that fundamentally requires promise keeping), some of which exclude the criterial property and entail its possession by an alternative (for example, 'breaking one's promise' in relation to the same principle). Otherwise, if the act is identified in ways that entail neither the absence nor the presence of the relevant criterial property, it is logically an open question whether the act is favoured or opposed by the principle; that depends on the further facts of the case. Consequentialistic principles are most often applied to acts that are identified in relatively neutral terms. It is logically an open question, for example, whether keeping or breaking one's promise, obeying or disobeying the law, and so on, are favoured or opposed by a principle that fundamentally requires promoting the community's happiness or everyone's.

Principles may be said to be 'contradictory' when it is logically guaranteed that they will not agree in their judgements, regardless of the facts; but these are not the principles that concern us here. We are concerned with principles that are simply *non-equivalent* in the sense that the criterial property of one does not entail the criterial property of the other. It is not necessarily the case that, if an act is favoured by one such principle, it will be favoured or, more important, will not be opposed by another such principle; it is possible for such principles to conflict in practice. If, now, we exclude 'contradictory' principles from this class, we can also say that they will not necessarily conflict either. Whether they conflict or harmonize in practice is logically an open question. This can also be seen as follows. An act is either identified in terms of the criterial property of one such principle or it is not. If not, then contingent assumptions must be made before any judgements about the act can be derived from the first principle. If the act is identified in terms of the first criterial property, then contingent assumptions must be made before any judgements about the act can be derived from the second principle. This is because the criterial properties of two non-equivalent principles are logically independent, neither entailing nor excluding the other. In other words, before it is possible for non-equivalent principles to yield inconsistent judgements about specific acts, contingent assumptions must be made. Such principles can conflict, but will not necessarily do so. The inconsistencies are not generated by the principles alone, but only by them in conjunction with certain factual, contingent premisses. It remains logically an open question, then, what should be given up—one of the principles or the factual beliefs.

My argument so far has been this. Even if we grant that non-equivalent principles can, under certain circumstances (or together with certain contingent, factual assumptions) lead to inconsistent judgements, it does not follow, and in fact it is false, that such principles are logically inconsistent. This sort of *a priori* argument against the co-acceptability of such principles will therefore not work, and it cannot be used against the dual-standard reading of Bentham.

But it might be objected that the two principles actually *do* conflict in practice and that one who subscribes to non-equivalent principles in a world in which they actually do conflict has committed himself to an untenable position. This objection may be answered in two ways. First, this still does not yield an *a priori* argument against supposedly conflicting principles, once it is granted that the mere possibility of conflict does not count against them. For actual conflict cannot be shown on *a priori* grounds. The critical issues are factual, the relevant facts are often unknown by anyone (indeed they are sometimes currently unknowable), and even in the simplest cases the alleged facts can honestly be contested. It may seem obvious that self-interest actually does sometimes conflict with community interest; but this cannot be shown without extensive, substantive argument from experience. This line of reasoning therefore does not lead to an *a priori* argument against the co-acceptability of non-equivalent principles. And it therefore cannot lead us to reject the dual-standard interpretation of Bentham.

Secondly, it would seem that, if our question is what principles can rationally be *subscribed* to, we must take into account not some supposedly independent facts constitutive of the actual world, but rather the relevant *beliefs* about the world that one may have. If the mere subscription to principles P and P' is not rationally indefensible, but can become indefensible somehow in virtue of fact F, then the question is not whether F is the case but whether F is believed to be the case by one who subscribes to P and P'. More precisely, the question is whether one can rationally fail to believe F. This may be true for some Fs, given certain other beliefs. But this cannot be used to show the untenability of Bentham's dual standard, for the requisite beliefs are *not necessarily* held.

I have assumed in all this that it would be irrational for a person to subscribe to non-equivalent principles P and P' in conjunction with belief in fact F, where F generates an actual conflict between the two principles. And this is because I have been granting that such combinations of principles and beliefs yield logical inconsistencies. But now I shall refuse to assume this any longer. Without entering into the matter very deeply, I believe we can see that non-equivalent principles can rationally be subscribed to even when it is supposed not only that they can possibly conflict, but that they actually do conflict in practice. If someone did not believe that his admittedly non-equivalent principles ever do conflict, then his moral world, so to speak, would be somewhat more comfortable and harmonious than the one that most of us seem to live in. If someone did believe that his principles sometimes conflict, his moral world would be like ours. In such a world, principles cannot always be fully satisfied. But I do not see why accepting this leads to an untenable position. A person with one single principle faces no such troubles; he believes that there is one and only one respect in which acts can be judged worthy and criticized. A person with two or more independent non-equivalent principles may lead a less comfortable moral life, but what logical penalties does he pay for that? He simply believes that there is more than one fundamental, irreducible respect in which acts can be judged worthy and criticized, and this is a perfectly intelligible position. Such a position *could* be made incoherent, to be sure, by supposing that a person with admittedly independent non-equivalent principles says of *each* that *it* is the only fundamental principle; that the different criterial property of each principle is the only basic respect in which acts can be made right; or that, come what may, each of his principles must always be fully satisfied. But the irrationality of such a person is not due solely to his subscribing to non-equivalent principles; it is like the irrationality of a person who has, and admits that he has, two distinct and different hands, and then declares that each hand is the only hand he has. It is not incumbent on one who subscribes to non-equivalent principles to take these further steps that would land him in absurdity.

How does all this apply to Bentham? In the first place, even if we suppose that the two parts of the dual standard actually conflict, the crucial question is whether Bentham *believed* they did. I shall argue later that Bentham, when he embraced the dual standard, did not entertain the possibility of a real conflict between the longterm interests of a single individual and the interests of his community. He therefore did not subscribe to those factual beliefs that would be required to form an inconsistent set with the dual standard (if any beliefs *could* have that effect). Bentham's assumptions about the natural harmony of human interests when he wrote the *Introduction* might strike us today as terribly naïve, but he cannot be convicted of a logical blunder on that account. His views were not atypical of his time,[1] and it is highly doubtful that he could be shown *irrational* for holding them. It seems unlikely that other beliefs of his would rationally have obliged him to accept the idea that personal and community interests substantially diverge. I shall argue that such a belief is not required, for example, by his theory of punishment—not, at least, when he wrote the *Introduction*.

Secondly, it is also important that Bentham did not literally embrace two independent principles in subscribing to a dual standard in the way I am suggesting. He conceived the dual standard as deriving from a more basic principle of utility, by virtue of two distinct types or spheres of application. One must therefore regard it in the following manner. Either the dual standard is as self-consistent as the principle from which it is supposed to derive, or else it isn't. If it is, there is no prima facie case against the interpretation, because there is no prima facie case against the consistency of a differential principle of utility. If the dual standard is not as self-consistent as the underlying principle, then that could only be because there is an error in the derivation which Bentham failed to detect. Now, I shall argue that there are in fact flaws in Bentham's suggested derivation of the dual standard, but these do not tend to show that the dual standard itself is inconsistent. Moreover, there are reasons for denying that the dual standard could be internally incoherent. The difficulty we have been considering arose because we assumed that the two standards have the same or at least some overlapping applications. But this, while initially plausible, may well be mistaken. Let us see why.

Principles of conduct usually apply to whatever a person may be said to do of his own accord, and the evidence shows that the principle of utility is no exception. Bentham says

[1] See Elie Halévy, *The Growth of Philosophic Radicalism*, tr. M. Morris (Faber & Faber, London, 1953), pp. 13–17.

that it applies 'to every action whatsoever', including not only 'every action of a private individual' but also 'every measure of government' (*IPML*, I, 2). For example, he clearly wants the principle to cover not only what he calls 'positive acts' but also 'negative' ones such as omissions and forbearances, even when the omission has not been contemplated by the agent (*IPML*, VII, 8, incl. note d).

One would suppose that what Bentham calls 'ethics at large' is the area covered by the principle of utility. The two subdivisions of ethics at large would seem to correspond to the two classes of act mentioned specifically by Bentham, namely, private acts and measures of government. If we ask how this division of ethics is to be understood, the following suggestion appears initially to be the most plausible. Private ethics, or the art of self-government, concerns whatever a person may be said to do of his own accord, and public ethics, or the art of government (in the ordinary sense), concerns every instance 'of a government functionary or set of functionaries exercising the powers of Government' (*IPML*, I, 1, note a), or in other words anything done by someone acting in his official capacity. This was implicitly the way we understood Bentham when we invited the charge of internal inconsistency against the dual standard.

Now, the line between what a public official does 'officially' and what he does 'privately' may be hard to draw, but the distinction seems valid none the less. But, no matter how we make the distinction, we seem forced to conclude that Bentham's private and public ethics overlap, and therefore that his two standards—one for each part of ethics—can conflict. For *whatever* a public official does in his official capacity is presumably also something that he does of his own accord, and this, specifically, is what gave rise to the original objection. There may be exceptions here, for an official can be forced in various ways to take or omit official action, and then he would not perhaps be acting 'of his own accord'; but these exceptions will not exhaust the class of official actions, and therefore some overlap between the two classes is assured, with room for conflict between the two standards.

This interpretation of Bentham's division of ethics may be mistaken, and small adjustments in it would segregate the two sectors and eliminate all possibility of conflict between the two standards. For example, one could define the public sector first and confine the private sector to the remainder of 'ethics at large'. In fact, this approach is implied pretty clearly in his *Chrestomathia*, one of the few places where he reverts to the partition of ethics.[2] The two sectors there are characterized as 'state-regarding' and 'not-state-regarding' ethics respectively. This way of describing the distinction makes the branches mutually exclusive. Now, we have no direct evidence that Bentham assumed this qualification when he originally drew up the division of ethics in the *Introduction*, but it does not seem unreasonable to apply it there. For its style conforms to his usual method (or ideal) of division into mutually exclusive and exhaustive parts, it would not alter his essential commitments, and it is the sort of qualification that one would expect made once it was found lacking. Given this way of drawing the distinction, 'inconsistency' could not become a problem for the dual standard, for the two parts of ethics would not overlap at all and the two standards would have no applications in common.

2. *Obligation and the Law*

Let us turn to the second problem for the dual standard. Suppose that an established legal rule satisfies the appropriate standard for legislation. (Depending on how we understand Bentham, we might say either that the rule itself promotes the community's happiness, or—as I think fits his position better —that the legislative behaviour involved in maintaining the rule promotes the community's happiness. The present argument can be developed on either approach, and we can assume for the sake of simplicity that both conditions are satisfied.) Even if the interests of individuals can be assumed to converge perfectly in the long run, laws that satisfy the appropriate standard do not necessarily serve those interests in each and every case. For the collection of interests is extremely complex, and laws cannot always take all of them fully into account. Legislators and administrators are finite creatures. Laws must be made simple enough for ordinary citizens to use in deciding

[2] Encyclopedical Table, Table V in Bowring, VIII, insert opp. p. 128. See also Bentham's commentary on pp. 93f.

what to do and for ordinary public officials to apply, and so they cannot necessarily make room for every twist and turn of human interest. A legal rule which satisfies the political half of the dual standard, therefore, can conceivably require some specific acts of members of the community that are not approved by the private half (not even when the risks of legal sanctions are taken into account). (I am assuming, of course, that what a private person decides to do falls within the realm of private ethics, even if some of his alternatives involve breaking the law; for otherwise the notion of a private ethics would be virtually empty. There is usually some law that a private person is in a position to comply or fail to comply with.) It follows that one who subscribes to a dual standard must be prepared to say that the political half can support a law that prohibits a certain act while the private standard favours breaking the same law by committing the act in certain specific conditions. And this may be regarded as a kind of moral inconsistency—or at least a morally paradoxical position. The difficulty is aggravated when we realize that the political standard could also be used to justify punishment of the same individual for his violation of the law, even when the private standard approves his act.

This type of case does not support a straightforward charge of 'inconsistency' against the dual standard, for directly conflicting judgements are not made about the same items; one single act, for example, is not called both right and wrong. But then the difficulty cannot be eliminated by segregating public and private ethics in the way I have suggested. Now, there does seem something paradoxical about a view which has consequences like those just sketched, but the difficulty might easily be exaggerated. It can be shown, in any case, that this problem does not affect the dual standard as an interpretation of Bentham's position, for basically the same points could be made about the other interpretations. But let us first put some complicating matters to one side.

The objection might seem more imposing than it really is if we assume that one is under a moral obligation to comply with a morally justified legal rule. For it might seem to follow that one could never be justified in disobeying that rule. But this would be mistaken. In judging a legal rule to be morally justified, one does not thereby commit himself to believing that he must do whatever it requires, regardless of the circumstances. For, even if the obligation stays in force, so to speak, it is possible that other, stronger moral considerations will 'outweigh' it. This is one of several important aspects of obligations: they have moral limits, they can often be extinguished, and they can sometimes be overridden.

If one accepts the idea that a moral obligation to obey a law follows from its being morally justified, then the most that might be claimed, in general, is that there is a non-trivial obligation to obey the law. By 'non-trivial' I mean, for a utilitarian, that one's obligation to conform to the rule is (so to speak) weightier than the utility of compliance with the rule, so that the obligation can outweigh the disutility of disobedience in particular cases. (If one is not prepared to say even this, then there is no point in his saying that one is under a 'moral obligation' to obey a morally justified law.) But to say this is not the same as saying that one must do whatever the rule requires, for special circumstances can conceivably arise in which such an obligation is outweighed.

Now, the sort of view just described, if it is held by any kind of 'utilitarian' at all, would be held by the type called a 'rule-utilitarian'. (I am restricting this label to those whose position represents a real, substantive alternative to the classic view that utility is the direct test for conduct.) He says, roughly, that one ought to act in accordance with rules that are themselves justified by their utility, and that acts themselves are not to be judged by their own utility when they are required or prohibited by such rules, except perhaps in very special circumstances. But it seems fairly clear that this is not Bentham's kind of utilitarianism. The existence of a justified (or unjustified) law, for example, makes a difference to action under it—but only as it affects the utilities of such actions. This does not commit Bentham to saying that one is under a non-trivial moral obligation to conform to justified rules. These facts about his position undercut the objection: they do not show that his position is correct, but make the objection irrelevant.

Confusion can be generated by Bentham's own views about the nature of obligations. He seems to say that to be under an obligation is to be required or forbidden to do something and to be threatened with sanctions for not complying. If we ignore extra-legal social sanctions, we can say that all obligations are therefore legal obligations, that is, are imposed and enforced by the law. Bentham also seems to say that laws are essentially 'obligative'. They require or forbid, and these 'commands' are backed by sanctions. All laws impose obligations. This commits Bentham to saying that anyone who comes under the province of a law is thereby under an obligation to do what the law requires.

There are several difficulties with this reconstruction. It is enough for us to note at this point that, even if the reconstruction were correct, the sense in which Bentham would be committed to saying that one is 'under an obligation' as a result of falling under a restrictive law would not commit him to the claim that one is under a non-trivial *moral* obligation to comply with a morally justified law. The argument would show only that Bentham is committed to so-called *legal* obligations under the law, and these have no relevant implications for morality. Unless one makes some further, logically independent assumptions—about the disutility of breaking laws, for example, and its consequent possible wrongness—one cannot say that being under such a legal obligation warrants even the slightest moral presumption in favour of obeying the law. (This is Bentham's position, and on this point he seems correct.) But the sense in which the original objection was raised concerned moral obligations under the law, moral presumptions in favour of obeying it.

In any case, competing interpretations of Bentham's utilitarianism would be subject to the same sort of objection, however cogent it may be. Suppose, for example, that we took Bentham to be a universalistic utilitarian. (We might just as well take him to be a parochialist; it makes no difference in principle to the argument.) He would still be faced with similar possibilities of divided judgements. For, from the fact that a legal rule satisfies the greatest happiness test, it does not follow that each and every act required by the rule could be justified by a *direct* application of the very same standard to the behaviour of the individuals coming under the rule. The same considerations apply here as before. Laws cannot always provide for every special circumstance and every twist and turn of human interest. And the difficulty faced by one embracing a dual standard would be no different in principle from the difficulty faced by one with a single standard which applies both to laws and directly to conduct falling under them. For it is a contingent question whether personal and community interests harmonize or conflict, so there is no logical presumption for saying that a utilitarian with a dual standard would be more likely than one with a single standard to justify individual acts of disobedience under laws that he nevertheless approves. If there is a paradox here, it accrues to all forms of utilitarianism (leaving aside rule-utilitarianism, which is irrelevant). It cannot be used to show that one variety is intrinsically more plausible than another. But since it seems quite clear that, even if utilitarianism as a general theory is not satisfactory, utilitarian considerations are valid and must be incorporated into any satisfactory moral theory, and since any such theory must likewise apply both to laws and to the conduct of individuals under them, this sort of difficulty may well be faced by any adequate theory whatsoever. There is an interesting moral problem here, but not one that divides moral theories into the prima facie plausible and implausible.

I conclude that the dual-standard interpretation of Bentham's utilitarianism cannot be rejected out of hand as untenable and that we must still consider it as a viable candidate. We shall proceed, therefore, to examine its textual support.

4

THE CONVERGENCE OF INTERESTS

1. The Problem of Evidence

IN Chapter 2 a new interpretation of Bentham's utilitarianism was proposed, based on his dual standard in the *Introduction* and attempting to account for it. I defended this proposal in Chapter 3 by arguing that Bentham could consistently have embraced both a standard of self-interest for private ethics and one of community interest for political affairs, even though the standards are not equivalent and might conceivably diverge. Now we must test this interpretive hypothesis against the most important textual evidence.

We shall concentrate upon the *Introduction*, for several reasons. It would be helpful to determine the position that Bentham takes in that book, for it is one of the few that he completed himself—it has not been modified to suit editors or collaborators—and it contains the fullest discussion of his utilitarianism. The *Introduction* might be used to help us understand Bentham's other works, but it would be much riskier to impose readings on that book based on most of the other writings that have appeared under his name. Moreover, we know that some of Bentham's views changed during his long career, and it is possible that some of those relating to his utilitarianism changed too, so we should hesitate before assuming that his later works agree with the *Introduction*. In fact, as we shall see, his beliefs about human selfishness hardened and he became less optimistic about the natural harmony of human interests, and these attitudes affect the interpretation of his utilitarianism.

One also finds that there is remarkably little evidence in Bentham's published work which might be used to challenge the new interpretation—at least, without the aid of highly debatable assumptions. This needs a little explaining. We have seen how Bentham uses the appropriate standard of community interest for political affairs in most of his writings, which generally concern such matters. In most places he explicitly states the standard in parochial terms, and elsewhere his superficially universalistic formulations might well be regarded as elliptical. This mass of evidence is ambiguous, however, for it could be used either to argue that Bentham has a parochial principle or in favour of the dual-standard interpretation. The crucial test for these competing interpretations would be whether Bentham uses the standard of self-interest for private ethics, as the new interpretation would lead us to expect. But, whether we confine ourselves to the *Introduction* or go beyond it, we can find little evidence that bears directly on this question. For Bentham was never much concerned with strictly private ethics, and the topics he chose to write upon gave him very few occasions for stating his relevant views. I have been able to discover a few relevant passages outside the *Introduction*, but I shall not discuss them further here.[1] Our chief concern is with the *Introduction*, and there is much of interest there.

Before we proceed, one comment ought to be made about apparent counter-evidence. Some passages in his work suggest a universalistic view, some passages a pure parochialism without a dual standard, and all of these might seem to undermine the new interpretation. But now we must be careful, for these two different kinds of counter-evidence are not mutually reinforcing. We are seeking a positive account of Bentham's posi-

---

[1] Evidence that Bentham's position may have been different in other works includes the following: (1) In the *Deontology* (ed. Bowring, 1834—after Bentham's death), the 'public happiness' is said to be the standard for private ethics (ch. II, par. 4; pp. 23f.). But there is some doubt of the text's complete authenticity, which can be seen in the passage in question, as 'public happiness' is an expression that Bentham rarely, if ever, uses. This book is of limited use for an interpretation of the *Introduction*, which, by contrast, was written some seventy years earlier and is known to be Bentham's own work. (2) In the *Principles of Penal Law*, it is suggested that 'the principle of general utility' requires benevolence extending to the whole of humanity (pt. II, ch. XVI; in Bowring, I, 563). But the import of these remarks is uncertain, for the text continues: 'The more we become enlightened, the more benevolent shall we become; because we shall see that the interests of men coincide upon more points than they oppose each other' (ibid.). Note also that 'the principle of general utility' is not a typical Benthamic expression, which is not surprising, for this work is the result of translations by third parties from Dumont's *Traités de legislation*, itself constructed by Dumont from Bentham's papers. (3) In *A Fragment on Government*, Bentham says that 'the obligation to minister to general happiness [is]

tion, and we therefore need a comparative assessment of the competing interpretations. We cannot be satisfied with saying that one reading fails to harmonize with certain passages; we need to see which reading best fits all the facts. None of the alternative accounts can be proved conclusively by the texts. I shall claim only that the dual-standard hypothesis, combined with the differential interpretation of his basic principle, is best supported by the texts—at least by that of the *Introduction*, the most important of Bentham's works.

2. *Private Ethics and the Art of Legislation*

Let us first consider the final chapter of the *Introduction*, specifically its first section, which supplied some of the passages on which the new interpretation was based (*IPML*, XVII, 2–4 and 20). We can deal with the main problems for this reading by concentrating on paragraph 8, where Bentham begins his discussion of the announced topic, the 'Limits between private ethics and the art of legislation'. The first half of this paragraph reads as follows:

> Now private ethics has happiness for its end: and legislation can have no other. Private ethics concerns every member, that is, the happiness and the actions of every member of any community that can be proposed; and legislation can concern no more. Thus far, then, private ethics and the art of legislation go hand in hand. The end they have, or ought to have, in view, is of the same nature. The persons whose happiness they ought to have in view,

---

an obligation paramount to and inclusive of every other' (ch. I, par. 36, note; in Bowring, I, 269). Note, however, that the *Fragment* (1776) antedates the *Introduction* by a few years. This may be important, for, as we shall see, one may speculate that Bentham's position in the latter work developed only in the process of its final drafting. Similar considerations affect the significance of the next item. (4) In the *Fragment* he also says (about the 'juncture for resistance' to established government): 'It is *then*, we may say, and not till then, allowable to, if not incumbent on, every man, as well on the score of *duty* as of *interest*, to enter into measures of resistance; when, according to the best calculations he is able to make, *the probable mischiefs of resistance* (speaking with respect to the community in general) *appear less to him than the probable mischiefs of submission*' (ch. IV, par. 21; in Bowring, I, 287). If this fell under public ethics, no difficulty would result from Bentham's apparent application of the community interest standard. But in the *Introduction* (XVII, 18, note s) he places it under private ethics. Even so, the position is unclear because of the explicitly assumed convergence of 'duty' and 'interest'.

as also the persons whose conduct they ought to be occupied in directing, are precisely the same. (*IPML*, XVII, 8)

It is possible for this to look more troublesome than it really is. Bentham says, for example, that private ethics and the art of legislation (a part of the art of government, or public ethics) both have 'happiness' as their proper end.[2] But, contrary to possible appearances, this does not preclude a dual standard, for he would apply the term 'happiness' not only to a particular individual but also to a community (the happiness or interest of which, as we have seen, he has already explained). Moreover, Bentham explicitly leaves room for the differences required by the dual standard when he says that their ends are, not identical, but 'of the same nature'. In a similar way, what Bentham says about the happiness and direction of everyone is compatible with the dual standard, for private ethics and the art of legislation are equally concerned with such things, although in somewhat different ways. (Some of these differences are, in fact, crucial to the argument of this paragraph.)

Bentham continues:

The very acts they [i.e. private ethics and the art of legislation] ought to be conversant about, are even in a *great measure* the same. Where then lies the difference? In that the acts which they ought to be conversant about, though in a great measure, are not *perfectly and throughout* the same. There is no case in which a private man ought not to direct his own conduct to the production of his own happiness, and of that of his fellow-creatures: but there are cases in which the legislator ought not (in a direct way, at least, and by means of punishment applied immediately to particular *individual* acts) to attempt to direct the conduct of the several members of the community. Every act which promises to be beneficial on the whole to the community (himself included) each individual ought to perform of himself: but it is not every such act that the legislator ought to compel him to perform. Every act which promises to be pernicious upon the whole to the community (himself included) each individual ought to abstain from of himself: but it is not every such act that the legislator ought to compel him to abstain from. (*IPML*, XVII, 8)

[2] cf. *A Fragment on Government*, Preface, par. 54; in Bowring, I, 237. The 'tendency' to 'happiness' is called 'utility' and the 'divergency' from it 'mischievousness'. But 'happiness' is also said to be what 'every man is in search of', 'the common end of all'. That passage, too, can be made coherent only if Bentham assumes the convergence of interests.

Bentham then goes on to explain, in the following paragraph:

Where then is the line to be drawn?—We shall not have far to seek for it. The business is to give an idea of the cases in which ethics ought, and in which legislation ought not (in a direct manner at least) to interfere. If legislation interferes in a direct manner, it must be by punishment. Now the cases in which punishment, meaning the punishment of the political sanction, ought not to be inflicted, have already been stated. If there be any of these cases in which, although legislation ought not, private ethics does or ought to interfere, these cases will serve to point out the limits between the two arts or branches of science. (*IPML*, XVII, 9)

Now, if one is seeking arguments against the dual-standard reading, he might grasp upon the second half of paragraph 8, where Bentham says that a 'private man' ought to do whatever is beneficial on the whole to the community and ought to refrain from doing what is pernicious to it. How could Bentham say this if his standard for private ethics were the agent's self-interest? If this seems impossible, the passage may be taken as showing that community interest is Bentham's single standard, for private as well as public affairs.

This objection leads to a parochial interpretation of Bentham's utilitarianism. But if we allow the assumptions that underlie the objection, then we can use the same passage to discredit the parochial interpretation too. For Bentham also says that a man ought always to serve *his own* interests (as well as those of his community). How could he say this if he had only a community interest standard?

The original objection and the retort make a common assumption, namely, that personal and community interests sometimes conflict, so that self-interest sometimes approves acts that go counter to community interest, and vice versa. But it is important to see that our question is not whether interests can so conflict, but Bentham's views about them. We can believe what we like about relations between personal and community interests, but if we wish to make any sense at all of this paragraph then we must suppose that Bentham assumed that the interests of a 'private man' converge, at least in the long run, with the interests of his community. Otherwise this passage would be incoherent, on either interpretation. If we take him to assume that interests naturally converge, then we can understand how he could say in effect that a man who serves his own happiness will always serve the happiness of his fellow-creatures, and vice versa. And if we allow Bentham this assumption, the objection to the dual-standard reading collapses, for Bentham could regard private ethics and the art of legislation as governed by two different standards and yet believe that they always lead, in practice, in the same direction.

This reading is not forced: it does not stretch any words, rely on special meanings, or any such thing. It simply imputes to Bentham a view about the harmony of human interests which was not unusual among writers on morals and politics during the period in which this book was written.

But the point needs further discussion, because it has surprising implications for his theories of punishment and human motivation. It will be easiest to deal with these matters by considering other objections that might be inspired by the passage in question.

3. The Basic Price of Legislation

Bentham has defined private ethics and the art of legislation (which is part of the larger art of government) in terms of the 'direction' of human agents. Private ethics, or the art of self-government, is concerned with the behaviour of a person when he is not influencing or controlling the behaviour of others (at least, not in his official capacity as a government functionary), while legislation concerns the direction of others. Bentham now wishes to contrast these areas in terms of 'the acts they ought to be conversant about'. But, as the argument of paragraph 8 makes clear, this is not simply a contrast between what a private person and a legislator ought to do. It is a contrast between what private ethics says that a man ought to do and what the art of legislation says that a man ought to be required or forbidden by law to do. Bentham's point is that not every act that private ethics says a man ought to do ought to be required by law, and not every act that private ethics says a man ought to refrain from doing ought to be prohibited. The factor that determines this difference is punishment, which inevitably involves 'mischief' (or disutility), and which is connected closely with legislation but not with private ethics.

Bentham is making a general theoretical point in paragraph

8 which concerns the *utilitarian* 'arts' of legislation and self-government. It is important to see that he is not drawing a sociological contrast between, say, actual law and conventional morality. For, just as these arts were originally defined (in paragraphs 2–4) from a utilitarian point of view, we have every reason to believe that they retain that special orientation in paragraph 8. Bentham is aware that both arts could be understood in non-utilitarian terms, but when he speaks of what they *ought* to do or what *ought* to be done under them, it is quite clear that he applies utilitarian criteria; and these criteria operate in the argument of paragraph 8.

Conventional morality, or the socially established and predominant values within a given society or group, would be identified by Bentham in terms of the 'moral or popular sanction', the informal social pressures which are to conventional values roughly as legal sanctions are to legal rules and requirements (*IPML*, III, 5). In Bentham's view, sanctions have a necessary connection with conventional morality. But they have no necessary connection with private ethics in the sense in which that term is used in the actual argument of paragraph 8. For there private ethics simply represents the implications of a utilitarian standard for ordinary private behaviour. And, from the fact that acts are to be approved or disapproved on the grounds of their utility, it does not follow that informal social pressures or any other sanctions will be brought to bear against one who threatens to deviate from those 'dictates' of utility. The very idea of a private ethics (understood as the utilitarian art of self-government) is distinct from that of conventional morality and, as Bentham rightly recognizes, the two sets of values do not necessarily agree, for the values accepted within a society at a given time do not necessarily conform to what utility approves. (See, e.g., *IPML*, VI, 41; cf. *Laws*, XVI, 12.)

This point is worth emphasizing because in paragraph 9, when Bentham indicates the relevance of legal punishment to his argument, he speaks not only of legislation 'interfering' in private behaviour, but also, apparently in a loose and misleading way, of private ethics 'interfering' too. This may suggest that when private ethics says what a man ought to do, social sanctions always support that judgement. But this cannot be what Bentham means. Moreover, and more importantly, sanctions are not *employed* as *instruments* by private ethics, in the way they are essentially employed by legislation, to back its requirements. All that the so-called 'interference' of private ethics need amount to is the possibility of making a judgement about what one ought to do on the basis of the relevant utilities.

Private ethics simply judges acts of ordinary individuals in their concrete circumstances. But legislation intervenes by *adding* sanctions to control and regulate such behaviour. Bentham clearly regards such regulation as the primary point of legislation, at least from a utilitarian point of view. As far as restrictive legislation is concerned, it must be backed by sanctions, and these must be punitive. We shall discuss the details of Bentham's views on these matters later, but the qualifications one may wish to add will not affect the present argument. In any case, in paragraph 8 Bentham regards punishment as an essential part of legal rules that are used to direct, control, or influence behaviour.

But legal sanctions inevitably involve 'mischief', and before they can be justified, we must be confident that the good they can do will outweigh such evil. 'Mischief' for Bentham is pain or the expectation or objective likelihood of pain, all of which must be considered when making Benthamic calculations, because we are supposed to take the likely consequences of acts and measures of government into account when judging them. Punishment is a mischief when it is painful or unpleasant, or when it is likely to be. It therefore creates mischief whenever it is threatened or expected and in so far as one runs the risk of suffering it. Everyone is exposed to such objective risks, and punishment works as a threatening mischief precisely when it might be effective as a deterrent (which Bentham thinks is its chief use). Many other mischiefs are caused by the legal authorization of punishments, some quite indirectly. This means that all restrictive legislation is costly and to some extent evil, from a utilitarian point of view, because it provides punishments for disobedience and this inevitably involves some mischief, These costs must always be considered by a utilitarian legislator. But private ethics itself has no sanctions, and so such complications do not affect it.

Given this background, we can understand Bentham's argument in the following way. An act need only be mischievous on the whole for private ethics to oppose it, but an act must be more than merely mischievous for legal interference to be warranted, because the mischief accruing to the interference itself must be outweighed by the good that it can do. It follows that there can be mischievous acts that ought *not* to be prohibited by law; by parity of reasoning it can be shown that some beneficial acts ought not to be legally required. This is the basic contrast drawn in paragraph 8.

In the paragraphs that follow, Bentham develops these conclusions further. In effect, he is arguing against the legal enforcement of morality, that is, of private ethics, even when it rests on utilitarian foundations. This is perfectly consistent with, and indeed required by, his utilitarianism. The queston whether there ought to be a law is always to be answered by considering the utility of the law (or of the relevant legislative behaviour), not simply by considering the utility of the conduct to be regulated. And, as we shall see, Bentham goes on to argue against so-called 'paternalistic' legislation, that is, legislation designed solely to protect those whose behaviour it restricts.

But now an objection is possible. If the costs of legal punishment are used in such a simple way to explain this difference between private ethics and the art of legislation, then the very same standard of utility must be applied to the two sectors of ethics. For the standard will determine what counts as 'mischief'; but the argument assumes that what counts as 'mischief' for private ethics also counts as 'mischief' for the art of legislation, and vice versa. And how can this be reconciled with the dual-standard reading? If different standards were employed—self-interest for private ethics and community interest for legislation, for example—then the relations between what private ethics approves or disapproves and what the legislator ought to require or forbid by law would be far more complicated than paragraph 8 would seem to imply. Disadvantage to any individual in a community will always be relevant under the utilitarian art of legislation which uses the standard of community interest. But if there are conflicts of interest, then an act that is mischievous on the whole from a self-interested point of view will not always be mischievous *on the whole* from the standpoint of community interest; for it may be beneficial to others to a greater extent.

This argument is interesting, but not because it raises any essentially new difficulties for the dual standard. Let us settle the main issue first. The objection takes Bentham to be assuming that the interests of different individuals conflict so that an act which is mischievous from a self-interested point of view is not always mischievous from the standpoint of community interest. But this assumption has already been discredited, for we have seen how the paragraph can satisfactorily be read only if we suppose that Bentham believed in the natural harmony of human interests. Bentham assumes that personal and community interests converge, so he is free to offer the same general account as was sketched above of the relationship between private ethics and the art of legislation, even if he has a dual standard. If mischief is assessed on the basis of the dual standard, the relevant differences between the mischief of an act from the two points of view would always be one of *degree*, never a change in quality, and the argument would not have to be substantially more complex. For Bentham's point concerns acts that can independently be judged by private ethics to be right or wrong; even though an act in one's own interest would also be in the community's interest, he argues, it may not be justified to require it by law; even though an act counter to one's interest would also run counter to the community's interest, it may not be justified to prohibit it.

This objection can therefore be dismissed. But matters should not be allowed to rest just there, for the objection should not be accepted on its own terms. The objection most immediately suggests a faulty picture of utilitarian reckoning about legislation. Let us begin there.

4. *Some Complexities of Legislation*
Bentham's marginal note for the paragraph in question says only that 'Every act which is a proper object of ethics is not of legislation' (*IPML*, XVII, 8). Given the context, this seems to mean that some acts opposed by private ethics should not be prohibited by law, and that some approved (or demanded) by private ethics should not be legally required. However, in

claiming that the relations between private ethics and the art of legislation are simply drawn in paragraph 8, the objection may suggest that Bentham is making a far stronger point, namely, that the acts approved and disapproved by private ethics are, respectively, proper sub-classes of the acts that are justifiably required and forbidden by law, and that punish-ment alone makes all the difference. But the note cannot be read this way, the passage does not imply it, and Bentham does not mean it. Two complications are worth noting briefly .

Bentham does not maintain that every act that can justifi-ably be prohibited or required by law would *independently* be opposed or approved by private ethics. This is not part of the argument of paragraph 8, and Bentham's more qualified view becomes clear just a few paragraphs later. He observes that private ethics could not possibly oppose infringements of legally enforceable property rights, for example, until there are laws that determine different persons' property (*IPML*, XVII, 18). There cannot even *be* a case of stealing, from the legal point of view, without such laws, so there cannot be a mis-chievous act under the description 'stealing' until the lines are drawn. This means that private ethics cannot judge stealing to be wrong independently of the law.

Bentham's point may seem to rest on the fact that without certain legal rules it is simply impossible to describe mischiev-ous behaviour in certain ways.[3] But the point is more general, namely, that an act which is mischievous given the existence of a legal rule need not be mischievous at all without it, so that the judgements of private ethics sometimes depend on the existence of the relevant laws. And this is not just because legal sanctions make it unprofitable to break the law. Consider the 'rule of the road'. Before and after a legally enforceable rule of the road exists, we can speak of 'driving right' and 'driving left'. The legal consequences of driving in one of those ways will be changed by the introduction of legal sanctions, but that is not enough to make us say that these words have changed their meanings. So we can describe the relevant behaviour in the *same* terms before and after the rule exists. But before the rule is established there might be no good utilitarian argument

---

[3] cf. John Rawls, 'Two Concepts of Rules', *Philosophical Review*, vol. 64 (1955), 3–32.

in favour of driving right or driving left, because, for example, there exists no regular practice of driving on one side or the other. Both ways of driving can be equally hazardous. Because of this, there can be a good utilitarian argument for legislation—that is, for creating a rule, which would prevent more mischief than the sanctions that support it would impose. In other words, it can make no utilitarian difference which one of these two rules we choose, while it makes a great deal of difference whether or not *one* of them is chosen and established. (If it makes no difference which rule is chosen, we could not say of one of them that it *ought* to be created; but we could say of each that it would be *justified* from a utilitarian point of view.) Once the rule exists, private ethics could approve compliance with it, and not simply because of the threat of punishment for disobedience. For if the sanctions are effective, a social practise of driving on one side of the road rather than the other will be created (or reinforced) and that mode of driving will accordingly be (other things equal) less hazardous than driving on the other side. The difference of utilities will be *brought about* by legal sanctions, but the sanctions themselves do not enter into the relevant calculations.

Bentham clearly sees this kind of point, and nothing in paragraph 8 denies it. He therefore does not hold—nor should he hold—that all the acts that are justifiably prohibited or required by law are independently opposed or approved by private ethics. The utilitarian legislator cannot proceed simply by enforcing some of the dictates of utility for private ethics, in view of the costs and effectiveness of punishments. He must also be creative, imagining socially useful arrangements that could be established.

It is also worth noting that punishment is not the only factor which Bentham believes determines the relations between private ethics and the art of legislation. It is an important one, and the point of paragraph 8 is made without considering any others. But Bentham discusses other factors too, the most important perhaps being that 'the legislator can know nothing' of particular individuals and their special circumstances (*IPML*, XVII, 15). The legislator should constantly remind himself how little he actually knows about the individuals who come under the scope of his sweeping laws, and what risks he takes—

or rather what dangers he exposes others to. Even when the
legislator only wants to serve those whose behaviour he res-
stricts, he should hesitate before legislating. For he is likely to
go wrong. In this section (*IPML*, XVII, 15–17) Bentham presents a clear case against unlimited paternalistic legislation,
one that anticipates the main line of Mill's much later essay
On Liberty.

5. *The Point of Punishment*

Our discussion has now touched upon Bentham's theory of
punishment, and it is time we looked into it more closely. It is
sometimes said that Bentham's rationale for legal punishment
rests on an assumption opposite to the one we have ascribed to
him. It presupposes that the interests of an individual often
conflict with those of his community. After all (it may be
argued), he believed that all men calculate, that they know
their own interests best, and that they always try to serve them.
Given these views, how could he think that punishment is
needed to goad men into doing what a utilitarian legislator
would require, if he also thought that the legislator, in serving
the interests of the community, also served the best interests of
each and every one of its members? If he believed in the
natural harmony of interests, then he would think that the
threat of punishment is needed only in rare and special cases,
as when a useful but sweeping general law fails to provide for
all the circumstances that fall under it (so that it requires some
specific acts that run counter to both the individual's and the
community's best interests). But the attention that Bentham
lavished on the topic of punishment and his view of it as essential to legislation seem to imply that it is needed quite often,
and that there is no natural harmony of interests among the
individuals within a given society. His idea must be that
punishment is needed to *create* an *artificial* harmony, so that
individuals while serving their own interests will be obliged
to serve the overall interest of the community too.[4] The threat
of punishment is added to *change* the interests of those who
come under the laws.

[4] cf., e.g., Halévy, *The Growth of Philosophic Radicalism*, pp. 17f., and
J. B. Schneewind, ed., *Mill's Ethical Writings* (Collier, N.Y., 1965), Introduction, 9.

This received interpretation is what I wish to deny. In some other works, Bentham suggests such a view.[5] But I only wish to claim that it is not expressed in, implied by, or required for the argument of his *Introduction*.

The account above involves some distortion of Bentham's actual views about human psychology. It represents Bentham as conceiving ordinary individuals as self-knowledgeable, self-centred, efficiently calculating agents. Now, it is true that Bentham says some things like those that the argument imputes to him, but his actual points are much more modest than the objection requires. He says, for example, that 'all men calculate', but he leaves considerable room for error. He does not suggest that we are generally excellent calculators. He simply wants to argue that it is useful to have rules for apportioning punishments to different offences, circumstances, and offenders, so that they can yield greater utility (*IPML*, XIV, 28). He also says that men know their own interests best—but only compared with others, most notably legislators. He explicitly allows that 'a man knows too little of himself' (*IPML*, XVII, 15). These modest points are compatible with the view that we are often blind to important longterm interests.

Bentham does not say that punishment must change our longterm interests. It is supposed to work by affecting our 'motives', our inclinations to behave one way or another, and thus by affecting our actual behaviour. Now, Bentham clearly thought that there is a special connection between our motives and our interests, but our motives are no simple function of our long range interests, and manipulating motives does not entail reversing our basic interests. Bentham's actual pronouncements on punishment and human psychology in the

---

5 See, e.g., (1) *The Rationale of Reward*, bk. I, ch. IV, par. 2; in Bowring, II, 199. Here Bentham discusses the possible meaning of 'two expressions . . . in familiar use with political writers', including 'the union of interest with duty', and does not clearly endorse the argument indicated in the text. (2) *Panopticon: Postscript, Part II*, sec. 2; in Bowring, IV, 125f. Here Bentham indicates the need to 'join interest with duty' by designing institutions appropriately. His concern is limited to controlling 'governors' by the prospect of profit. (3) *Tracts on Poor Laws and Pauper Management*, in Bowring, VII, 380. Here he mentions the '*Duty* and *Interest* junction principle', and envisages the use of punishments to effect this result, though he rejects such means for the case at hand. His concern is limited to control of the managers of an institution. (4) See text below for a discussion of the *Constitutional Code*.

Introduction are all compatible with the view that there is a natural harmony of human interests in the long run.

Or do Bentham's arguments for limiting paternalistic legislation suggest the opposite? For his point seems to be that, while we need laws and sanctions to support the rules of 'probity' (which forbid us to hurt others) and 'beneficence' (which require us to help them), we need none for the rules of 'prudence' (*IPML*, XVII, 15–19). How could he say this unless he thought that interests conflict? Well, first of all, interests of different individuals can *appear* to conflict without actually doing so. Secondly, legal sanctions might be needed to redirect behaviour chiefly when the interests of others are most directly affected but one's own interests are affected only indirectly. Thirdly, there is much for legislators to do that falls under none of these headings. We have already seen this illustrated in the rule of the road. The establishment of such a rule would serve all the members of the community, but it could not be counted as the legal enforcement of, say, prudence. The assumption of a natural harmony of interests is therefore compatible with Bentham's account of punishment.

6. *Psychological Egoism*

But the main error in the received interpretation of Bentham's rationale for punishment is that it pictures Bentham as a 'psychological egoist', one who holds that we all try to serve our own interests without a thought for others (except as we think that they are obstacles to or instruments for reaching our own private ends). It is dogmatic that Bentham conceived of human nature as selfish. But this dogma, like many others, is ill-founded.

I have already argued, in more than one way, that Bentham's psychological views are logically independent of his utilitarianism. This can be shown in another way, by considering a further objection to the dual-standard reading, based on the claim that Bentham was a pyschological egoist. On that assumption, one might argue that a private ethics based on self-interest would have no point, for it would only tell us all to do what we try to do regardless, namely, pursue our own happiness. And the requirement for public ethics, that legislators should serve the general happiness, would suffer the opposite fate. For it could not be followed (except coincidentally) if men were egoistic, because legislators, like all other men, would always be preoccupied with their own affairs.

But an egoistic pschology is compatible with the idea that private ethics should be governed by the standard of self-interest. And Bentham makes clear that he is not proposing any change in the standard underlying our private deliberations. 'In all this', he says, 'there is nothing but what the practice of mankind, wheresoever they have a clear view of their own interest, is perfectly conformable to' (*IPML*, IV, 8). Bentham is trying to make us better aware of our real, longterm interests, how they relate to the interests of others, how to assess them effectively. He wishes us to make our everyday calculations as knowledgeable and rational as possible. The point of all this is the more readily seen once we appreciate how imperfect our actual deliberations and self-knowledge appear to Bentham.

But Bentham's main interest is legislation, and here we can see at once that an egoistic psychology would pose a threat to the dual-standard reading if, and *only* if, it posed a similar threat to the competing interpretations. For all of these see Bentham as requiring legislators to promote the happiness of others, not just their own. It follows that the present objection cannot possibly make the dual-standard reading any less tenable than the others. Moreover, if someone is impressed by the imagined conflict between Bentham's utilitarianism and his allegedly egoistic psychology, he may conclude that Bentham assumes a natural harmony of human interests. But once that point is granted the overall objection collapses.

Despite all this, however, it is worth pursuing Bentham's philosophical views about human psychology a bit further, for the usual account is both popular and almost certainly wrong.

Bentham's views about human psychology, as well as moral theory, stand closer to Hume's than to Hobbes's, and it is plausible to suppose that Hume's influence was as considerable in the former case as we know it was in the latter. Hobbes is usually taken as saying that all our actions are essentially egoistic and that all appearances to the contrary can be explained away.[6] (Like most psychological egoists, Hobbes concentrated on debunking altruism and ignored the formidable

6 See *Leviathan*, ch. VI.

difficulties, for his view, of malevolence and masochism.) Hume admitted that the metaphysical simplicity of the Hobbesian theory gave it some philosophical appeal, but he thought that this was outweighed by the complex and implausible explanations that would be required to explain away unselfish behaviour. Hume thought that belief in unselfishness is better justified than acceptance of Hobbes's tortured explanations. He also argued that our shared morality, even our common moral language, implies a certain degree of unselfishness, for it presupposes some identification with the interests of other persons. Hume thought that each of us, to some degree, takes a sympathetic interest in the welfare of other persons—not because we expect to profit from their subsequent reactions, but simply because we identify with their interests, at least to some extent.[7]

This was also Bentham's view when he wrote the *Introduction*, and perhaps for some time thereafter. This is shown, for example, by his quite explicitly maintaining that we all have what might be called non-egoistic interests in the welfare and happiness of others; and he acknowledged the existence of antipathies as well as sympathies too. Of course he recognized that one can profit from helping and not hurting other people, who are likely to return our treatment of them in kind. These considerations dominate his late *Deontology*; but they are unimportant in his early *Introduction*. In any case, acceptance of them does not undermine his separate claim, that one can have interests in others which are independent of one's expectation of subsequent benefits. Bentham held that we have these other-regarding interests, and he nowhere maintains that they must be reduced to or grounded in beliefs about our own personal welfare.[8]

It is illuminating in this connection to trace a change in Bentham's views about human selfishness. His actual writings during most of his career manifest no clear commitment to an egoistic conception of human nature. But we find something like it in one of his last major works, the *Constitutional Code* (the relevant parts of which were completed, however, by Ben-

---

[7] See, e.g., *Enquiry Concerning the Principles of Morals*, sec. 6 and Appendix II.

[8] *Introduction*, e.g., V, 10–11, 26, 32; VI, 20–2, 26–7; X, 25, 36–8; XI, 11, 24.

tham's editors after his death). This is the only place that I
have been able to find in which he makes an explicit general
statement that might be construed as endorsing psychological
egoism, and the only place where his argument seems to assume
such a position.

The question arises when Bentham states the principles
upon which the work is to be based. The first is introduced as
follows:

The right and proper end of government in every political
community, is the greatest happiness of all the individuals of
which it is composed, say, in other words, the greatest happiness of
the greatest number. (Bowring, IX, 5)

But Bentham contrasts this 'right and proper end' with the
end that governments actually pursue:

The *actual* end of government is, in every political community,
the greatest happiness of those, whether one or many, by whom the
powers of government are exercised. (Bowring, IX, 5)

The reason for this, and for the possible conflict between the
right end and the actual end of a government, is what Bentham calls the predominance of self-preference, which he explains as follows:

By the principle of self-preference, understand that propensity
in human nature, by which, on the occasion of every act that he
exercises, every human being is led to pursue that line of conduct
which, according to his view of the case, taken by him at the
moment, will be in the highest degree contributory to his own
greatest happiness, whatsoever be the effect of it, in relation to the
happiness of other similar beings, any or all of them taken together.
(Bowring, IX, 5)

Now, one who believes that men are so constituted would
surely qualify as a psychological egoist. But it is interesting to
note that Bentham refrains from endorsing so pessimistic a
view. The evidence for self-preference is empirical, he says,
based on the history of nations and the survival of the race. He
admits that the egoistic thesis could be taken as an incontrovertible 'axiom', but he says that it need not be given that
special status. And he does not need so strong a premise to
make his intended point. His general purpose is to lay down

I.I.G.—6

guidelines for the structure of government and for legislation generally, and he believes that in this context it makes no difference whether we suppose that men are always selfish or that they are selfish only in the 'bare majority' of cases. He thinks it clear that self-preference is 'predominant', and he concludes that our institutions should be designed from the ground up on the assumption that self-preference is universal. The argument seems to place excessive weight upon risks as opposed to possible gains, and one could easily challenge it. But one can hardly question the fact that it is used by Bentham (Bowring, IX, 5–6).

Bentham is unwilling to commit himself to a view about self-preference that is any stronger than this: 'In the general tenor of life, in every human breast, self-regarding interest is predominant over all other interests put together' (Bowring, IX, 5). Self-preference generally predominates, but not always. Bentham allows the possibility of very many exceptions. When he finally comes to state a clear general position on the matter, then, he does not adopt a strictly egoistic conception of human nature.

And it is equally important to observe that this qualified egoism represents a conscious departure from his earlier lack of any clearly thought-out position. For Bowring reports Bentham's statement that it took him sixty years to comprehend the widespread hostility to the utilitarian doctrines he had advanced in *A Fragment on Government*. Bentham's diagnosis may be mistaken, but he claims that he finally recognized the cause to be the principle of self-preference, of which he said he had no 'clear perception' until late in his career.[9]

The emergence of this limited belief in human egoism appears to have accompanied his recognition that the interests of different individuals might conflict. This possibility, he explains in the *Code*, is the reason why he needs to say 'the greatest happiness of the greatest number' rather than 'the greatest happiness of all the members of the community', if his formula is to 'serve for all occasions' (Bowring, IX, 5–6). For

[9] *Memoirs*, Bowring, X, 80. But the time-span given is questionable, for the memoir is dated 1822 while the *Fragment* was published only forty-six years before. However, sixty years passed between the start of Bentham's utilitarian writings and his death in 1832, when he left the *Constitutional Code* unfinished.

the possibility of such conflict provides occasion for self-preference to operate. While Bentham failed to see this possibility, he
could equally fail to recognize what he later took to be self-
preference.

But even in the *Code*, where Bentham's psychological egoism
finally takes shape, it seems to concern him chiefly as a problem
about those govern*ing* rather than those govern*ed*. He recognizes that interests can be manipulated by the use of punishments (as well as by the limitation of governmental powers)
but he does not use human self-centredness and the possibility
of conflict as the basis for punishment *in general*. He uses it
only in connection with his concern for 'bringing the particular interest of rulers into accordance with the universal interest' (Bowring, IX, 6).

If one reads the *Code* out of context, one might mistakenly
project its views upon the much earlier *Introduction*. But we
have good reason to believe that Bentham's belief in human
selfishness and his recognition that interests do not naturally
harmonize arose late in his career. As far as he was concerned,
he had not been committed to an egoistic psychology when he
wrote the *Introduction*. Nor was he committed to the corresponding rationale of punishment. But he *was* committed to the
idea of a natural harmony. Bentham's testimony about his
change of attitude fits the most natural reading of his *Introduction* as well as his other major works on human psychology.

7. *Bentham's Hedonism*

In the light of these revelations, one might wonder why Bentham should so generally be regarded as a psychological egoist.
Now, it may be granted that his remarks are sometimes those
we would expect from one with an egoistic view of man. But in
fact there are very few such comments and, unless we came to
them with certain expectations, we would not be likely to place
much weight on them. Our background assumptions about
Bentham's views are undoubtedly a consequence of his 'psychological hedonism', his belief that all human action is determined by pleasure and pain. For such views are usually
classified as, and are usually meant to be, specific forms of
psychological egoism (on the assumption that the pleasures
one seeks and the pains one tries to avoid are always one's own).

It may therefore be assumed—it undoubtedly has been
assumed—that Bentham's hedonistic theory of human motivation entailed an egoistic conception of human nature. Even
if egoism followed from Bentham's hedonism, this would still
be compatible with my claims so far, provided that Bentham
was unaware of any such commitment. And we have just seen
that he recognized no commitment of this type for most of his
career. But I believe it is also true that Bentham's hedonism
was not meant to have such implications and probably had
none at all.

A variety of claims might be classified under the heading
'psychological hedonism', but the most important one is the
hedonic theory of goals. This is the view that all of one's desires and aversions—all of one's values—are reducible to the
desire for pleasure and the aversion to pain. According to this
theory, if I think that I will get more pleasure out of X than Y,
then I will seek X rather than Y; the contrary applies to pains.
One's desires are supposed to vary with the degree of pleasure
anticipated and inversely with the amount of pain expected.
And if one adds that one's actions are a function solely of the
strength of one's desires, then one has a hedonic theory of
human action as well as motivation.

Bentham holds some such view, and he can therefore seem to
be a psychological egoist.[10] But how does this fit in with his unqualified acceptance of non-egoistic motivations and desires?
And if he had such a view of human motivation, why would it
be necessary—how could it be possible—for him later to be
converted to the opinion that human beings are generally
selfish?

Bentham may have been confused on these matters, but it is
also possible that he had a slightly looser hedonic theory of
goals in mind. One might say, for example, that our desires are
always for pleasures and our aversions are always to pains, but
not insist that the pleasures and pains must be *our own*. The
prospect of bringing pleasure to another might attract us, for
its own sake, and cause us to behave accordingly; so could the
possibility of preventing another person's pain. It is important

10 Bentham's theory of motivation is developed most fully in the *Introduc-*
tion in X, esp. 2–9 and 43; see also VI, 1–4. cf. *A Table of the Springs of Action*,
in Bowring, I, 195–219.

to be clear about this, for it may be assumed that one expects to get pleasure from achieving his goals and pain from frustration. That still would not make non-egoistic motivation or action impossible, for it need not be the case that one wants to serve others *because of the pleasure one gets from it*; one might get pleasure from serving others *because one wants to serve them*. If one simply desires to serve others, that desire is not egoistic. Bentham acknowledges such desires without suggesting that they are egoistic, and they can be accommodated to a looser hedonic theory of goals. The object sought would still be pleasures and the objects avoided pains; but they would not always be pleasures and pains of one's own.

Matters are not quite so simple for Bentham, however, for he must also allow for antipathetic motivation, the implications of which he seems never to have considered seriously. In such cases one seeks to bring pain upon another or to prevent him from obtaining some pleasure. This can be made compatible with a loosened, non-egoistic hedonic theory of goals, but there are different ways of doing it. The details need not be pursued any further here. It is enough to recognize that by defining goals in terms of pleasure and pain we do not *thereby* commit ourselves to an egoistic psychology. Other assumptions associated with the hedonic theory of goals, but independent of it, are likewise neutral with respect to egoism; for example, the idea that one gets (or expects to get) pleasure from goal achievement, or that the thought of a pleasure is pleasant and the thought of a pain is painful.

A more important point is that the hedonic theory of goals is not the sole element in Bentham's hedonistic theory of motivation, and it may not be the most important part. An equally central idea is that of hedonic causation, the doctrine that pleasant and unpleasant thoughts are the most immediate *causes* of behaviour. Roughly speaking, the view is that I have a tendency to do something to the degree that my current thought of doing it, or of its consequences, is itself pleasurable, and that I have a tendency to act otherwise if my current thought is unpleasant. A view like this is not essentially egoistic because it leaves entirely open what thoughts of mine are pleasant or unpleasant. It does not imply that anyone is ever self-centred.

Bentham thinks of himself as working towards a mechanistic science of human behaviour in the Newtonian tradition, and in this respect his idea of hedonic causation is the crux of his theory. He believes that the 'will' is determined by antecedently existing 'motives', much as effects are temporally preceded by their causes, and that these motives are either pleasant or unpleasant thoughts. The hedonic theory of goals *adds* to this view by saying what these thoughts are *about*— what their crucial content is. But it is independent of the idea of hedonic causation.

The hedonic theory of goals assumes importance when Bentham applies his psychological doctrines to the problems of legislation. Pleasures and pains are supposed to be the only instruments that legislators (or anyone) can use for directing behaviour (*IPML*, III, 1; IV, 1). This can be done chiefly by threatening punishment for diobedience. In saying this, given his theory of hedonic causation, Bentham clearly assumes that the prospect of pain is painful, and this is why he thinks it can serve as a deterrent. He also seems to hold that pleasures are attractive—which means that the prospect of pleasure is pleasant.

Bentham's total view about motivation combines many hedonic elements, which are not all developed in complete detail. The ambiguous state in which he leaves them no doubt allows him to believe that non-egoistic motivation is perfectly possible.

We are now in a position to consider the passage in the *Introduction* which seems most clearly to express egoistic views. Bentham says that 'the only interests which a man at all times and upon all occasions is sure to find adequate motives for consulting, are his own' (*IPML*, XVII, 7). Interestingly enough, this remark is found in the paragraph immediately preceding the one in which he begins to draw the contrast between private ethics and the art of legislation—where, as we have seen, either his thoughts are hopelessly confused, or he assumes a natural harmony of human interests.

Now, from any standpoint, paragraph 7 is one of the most difficult to understand in the entire *Introduction*. For various independent reasons, it gives the impression of being carelessly drafted. But, given its context, it would seem that Bentham is arguing that private ethics, like legislation, supports the general requirements of probity and beneficence (our so-called 'duties' towards others) as well as those of prudence (the 'duty' to oneself). Bentham rests his case on the claim that all men are moved by 'social' motives such as sympathy. Men are just naturally concerned—at least to some degree—about the happiness of others. The argument seems intended to show how prudence in a subtle way requires that we discharge our duties of probity and beneficenec because, since we have these interests in others' welfare, we shall be made unhappy if we hurt or fail to help them. In other words, we have interests in their welfare that are antecedent to and independent of our fear of their retaliation and our hope for their goodwill. Bentham ignores the effect of antipathy and thus the argument seems inconclusive—unless (as is quite possible) he simply wants to show that we have *some* reason based on self-interest to perform our so-called duties towards other persons, even if that reason is not conclusive.

How, then, should we understand his remark that 'the only interests which a man at all time and upon all occasions is sure to find adequate motives for consulting, are his own'? There are various possibilities. One is that Bentham has found a con-fused way of making the trivial point that our interests are always our own—whatever their content. Another, similar to his point in the much later *Code*, is that we must assume that men are generally self-centred. This would be compatible with the idea of non-egoistic motivation, on the assumption that non-egoistic motives cannot generally be expected to be as strong as self-regarding ones. This is the more likely interpre-tation, except that it conflicts with the testimony that Bowring says we have from Bentham himself, that he did not come to such a view until considerably later.

Whatever we conclude about this single egoistic remark, however, it seems clear that Bentham does not deduce it from his hedonism, any more than he deduces his egoistic conclu-sions in the *Code*. His hedonistic theory of motivation seems separate from any egoistic tendencies.

One final remark about this passage should be made. If my reading of it is correct (and it can be defended on purely textual grounds), it reinforces the dual-standard interpreta-

tion of Bentham's utilitarianism. For Bentham sees the need
to argue that private ethics supports our duties towards other
persons, just as legislation is assumed to do, while he sees no
need to argue the point for legislation and offers no such argument. None is needed for legislation, for it is supposed to be
governed by the standard of community interest, and the relevant implications are obvious. If private ethics were governed
by the same standard, the argument of paragraph 7 would be
equally unnecessary. Bentham provides an argument precisely because his private ethics is based on self-interest.

8. *Acts Conformable to Utility*

The foregoing discussion of Bentham's psychological and social
views arose out of some passages that might seem, at first glance,
to conflict with the dual-standard interpretation of the *Introduction*. We have seen that troublesome readings can be given
to several passages, but that these collapse under closer examination. To complete our survey of the main evidence supplied
by the *Introduction*, we shall now turn briefly to its first chapter. In order of appearance in the text, the initial threat to the
dual-standard reading actually occurs shortly after the early
paragraphs (*IPML*, I, 2–4) on which that reading is partly
based. The passage in question appears more recalcitrant the
closer one looks at it.

In paragraph 6 of Chapter I Bentham says:

An action then may be said to be conformable to the principle
of utility, or, for shortness sake, to utility, (meaning with respect
to the community at large) when the tendency it has to augment
the happiness of the community is greater than any it has to diminish it. (*IPML*, I, 6)

This paragraph seems to leave no room for a dual standard;
it seems to say that community interest is the single, basic
standard of utility. Similar suggestions may be found in paragraphs 7–9.

Before we scrap the new interpretation, however, we should
recall the strength of evidence that led to it. This obvious
reading of paragraph 6 causes difficulties not just for the dual
standard but for the coherence of this chapter and the book as
a whole. In such a case one might throw up his hands, conclude

that Bentham was inconsistent, and give up the search for a satisfactory interpretation. But that should be the last resort. One might also look for ways of accommodating troublesome passages, so long as they are not distorted beyond recognition. Let us see whether this passage can be read any differently.

Consider the context. After his introductory paragraph (*IPML*, I, 1), Bentham states his principle of utility (paragraph 2) and then defines utility itself (paragraph 3). In so doing he employs the expression 'the happiness of the community', which he regards as misleading, at least from a metaphysical point of view. This is Bentham's first opportunity in the *Introduction* for applying his theory of linguistic fictions[11] and, since it concerns what is to him a most important notion, he does not let it pass. He therefore proceeds to explain what the interest of a community is, namely, 'the sum of the interests of the several members who compose it' (*IPML*, I, 4). He accordingly explains the interest of an individual, in terms of pleasure and pain (paragraph 5). The troublesome passages follow.

The issue comes down to this. The objection assumes that in paragraph 6 Bentham returns to his discussion of utility in general. If so, the new interpretation is threatened. But another possibility is that in paragraph 6 Bentham continues the discussion, begun in paragraph 4, of the particular species of utility that concerns an entire community. If so, the present objection collapses. Now, we cannot decide the issue just by looking at paragraph 6 alone, for it can be read in either way. The crucial element is Bentham's parenthetical remark, 'meaning with respect to the community at large', which qualifies 'utility', and which he might have inserted *either* to indicate that utility always concerns the community at large *or* that the immediate point concerns utility of that type. That he should make special remarks about this type of utility would be understandable, since most of the book concerns political affairs. The objection therefore seems inconclusive at best. But, if we take very seriously Bentham's explicit account of utility in general in paragraph 3, we must prefer the second

[11] His fullest treatment of this topic in the *Introduction* occurs at XVI, 25, note e2. cf. *A Fragment on Government*, ch. V, par. 6, note; in Bowring, I, 292f.; and *Bentham's Theory of Fictions*, ed. C. K. Ogden.

reading, the one compatible with the dual standard, for Bentham has in effect denied that utility always concerns the entire community. Sometimes, he says, it concerns only 'a particular individual' (*IPML*, I, 3). The objection therefore seems to fail, in the larger context of the passage.

But a more serious difficulty now faces us. If paragraph 6 is to harmonize with the new interpretation, then the actions referred to there cannot come under private ethics, because the standard applied is the happiness of the community, while the standard for private ethics should be self-interest. The acts in question must be political, and a defender of the dual-standard reading is obliged to suppose that when Bentham says 'action' here he means something like 'political action', or conduct within the scope of public ethics. The need to make such a significant insertion is discomforting enough; but the next paragraph makes the passage more troubling still:

A measure of government (which is but a particular kind of action, performed by a particular person or persons) may be said to be conformable to or dictated by the principle of utility, when in like manner the tendency which it has to augment the happiness of the community is greater than any which it has to diminish it. (*IPML*, I, 7)

Bentham makes the same point, once about 'actions', then about 'measures of government', in almost identical terms, in two successive paragraphs. But we have already been obliged to suppose that the 'actions' of paragraph 6 are political. If one supposes that 'measures of government' are simply political actions under a different name, then we have Bentham unaccountably repeating himself. This seems implausible—at least compared with the alternative possibility, that Bentham is talking about ordinary (not political) actions in paragraph 6 and about political acts, or measures of government, in paragraph 7. He would then be emphasizing a point he insists upon but otherwise makes only in passing, namely, that his principle applies not only to the private acts of ordinary individuals but also to the official conduct of government 'functionaries' (*IPML*, I, 1, note a; cf. I, 2).

The dual-standard reading of these paragraphs therefore burdens Bentham with redundancy. The only way to avoid this is to suppose that paragraphs 6 and 7 are not about the very same items; for example, that Bentham has an as yet un-explained distinction between political acts in general (the subject of paragraph 6) and measures of government (the sub-ject of paragraph 7). Now, even if Bentham had such a distinc-tion, there seems no reason to allude to it here, while there would be far more reason to explain it in the appropriate place (which he fails to do). But it is interesting to note that on en-tirely independent grounds we shall have reason to conclude that Bentham had such a distinction, which is needed for his derivation of the dual standard from the more basic principle of utility. The point of the distinction will become clearer when we discuss the matter more fully in the next chapter, but it may be explained briefly as follows. Bentham's principle applies pre-eminently to acts, to what is done or can be done by ordinary individuals. Now, acts are usually ascribed to human persons, and sometimes to them alone. But Bentham does not restrict his idea of an action so narrowly. As we have already seen, he includes animals in the class of 'agents', and thus he suggests that they too can act (*IPML*, XVII, 4). Acts can also be ascribed to personified entities, such as corporations and governments, which are not ordinary mortals, but may be treated linguistically as if they were individual persons. We shall see that Bentham is prepared to talk in such ways, and also that his derivation of the dual standard requires him to ascribe acts to governments as a whole, as distinct from public officials. I suggest, therefore, that these acts of governments as a whole are Bentham's 'measures of government' (understood as things that a government *does*, as opposed to, say, legal rules which result from its corporate behaviour). The class of such acts would not be identical with, nor even a proper sub-class of, ordinary political actions, performed by human persons, not even if we restrict the latter to functionaries behaving in their official capacities. Bentham would agree, of course, that anything a government can be said to do must either consist in or be analysable in some way in terms of the acts of ordinary individuals, so he would hold that the two classes are closely related. But they are also distinct. It is possible that some 'measures of government' are identical with the actions of specific government functionaries; for example, when a prime minister is empowered to act for his nation as a whole. At other times, and in general, however, they would not be identical with such ordinary acts, or with simple sums of them. The actions of collective bodies such as legislatures would be analysable in terms of, but would not be identical with, the actions of single individuals. And other types of governmental measures would probably need more complex modes of analysis.

Given this distinction, one possible way of reading these paragraphs makes Bentham talk about political acts, or the ordinary things done by real government functionaries in their official capacities, in paragraph 6, and about measures of government, or the things done by the state as a whole, in paragraph 7. Both kinds of action, Bentham says, must be judged by the standard of community interest. This is compatible with the dual-standard interpretation.

I am prepared to grant that this reading of paragraph 6 appears forced. But it must be assessed as part of an overall interpretation, compared with the alternatives. And any dissatisfaction that it causes is itself instructive, for there is no other place where so conjectural a reading must be given to a passage in order to defend the dual-standard interpretation. In other places, as we have seen, troublesome readings are available, but they simply do not stand up against general interpretive constraints as well as do those required by the new interpretation.[12]

---

[12] One final item may be noted. In ch. IV Bentham discusses the 'value of a lot of pleasure or pain', and presents what is often called his 'hedonic calculus'. The seventh factor on Bentham's list is 'extent'; 'that is, the number of persons to whom it [i.e., the class of pleasures and pains caused by a given act] *extends*; or (in other words) who are affected by it' (par. 4). This may make it appear as if Bentham wants us always to consider everyone who is affected by an act; but this does not follow. The 'method' is to be used for political as well as private ethics and so must include extent. The same accounting procedure would be used in private matters, except that extent would be excluded. This seems in fact to be illustrated by Bentham in his discussion of an example that clearly falls within private ethics (*IPML*, IV, 8). All factors save extent are mentioned there, but there is no indication that others' interests might not be affected.

A note appended to the second edition contains the following verses, 'framed in the view of lodging more effectually, in the memory, these points, on which the whole fabric of morals and legislation may be seen to rest':

9. How the Argument Now Stands

In this chapter I have examined the most important textual evidence that might be used to challenge my hypothesis that Bentham embraced a dual standard in the *Introduction*—community interest for political affairs, and self-interest for private matters. I have shown how this claim leads us to reconsider other beliefs and doctrines ascribed to Bentham, and how some dogmas must be surrendered.

My approach so far implies that these claims will be resisted. This is understandable. But how is it possible that the relevant evidence should have been misread by commentators, critics, and followers of Bentham? Various possible factors may be suggested.

Even if Bentham's political parochialism were recognized, the fact that he had a dual standard could easily be obscured because his preoccupation with political affairs left him few occasions for stating or applying the standard for private ethics. But it is worth noting some of the factors that might have prevented even his parochialism from being recognized.

Most of his political concerns fall within domestic politics, and it seems commonly (though erroneously) to have been assumed that external interests are not likely to be affected by the way such matters are resolved. If this assumption is made, then, given an agreement on the relevant facts, a universalist would be likely to draw the same conclusions that Bentham reached on the basis of his political parochialism. The fact that Bentham fails to consider the effects of his proposals on those outside the community in question would not seem to suggest that his political principles are parochial.

Some of Bentham's best-known formulations of the principle of utility (such as his informal statement of it in the *Fragment*,

---

Intense, long, certain, speedy, fruitful, pure –
Such marks in *pleasures* and in *pains* endure.
Such pleasures seek, if *private* be thy end :
If it be *public*, wide let them extend.
Such *pains* avoid, whichever be thy view :
If pains *must* come, let them *extend* to few. (*IPML*, IV, 2, note a)

Lines 1–4 suggest that extent is reserved for public ethics; but lines 5–6 muddy the waters by suggesting that extent is considered for pains in both public and private ethics, though not for pleasures.

Preface, paragraph 2) are not overtly parochial, which can be misleading. On the other hand, his 'explicit and determinate account' of it in the *Introduction* is, taken by itself, somewhat obscure in meaning. If the reader expects to find universalism there, he may read it in that way—or do what seems more usual, ignore that formulation altogether. For one cannot understand that statement of the principle without looking in an unlikely place, the final chapter of the book, which has obviously been neglected. It is therefore not surprising to find the only writer who quotes the 'explicit and determinate account' never mentioning the division of ethics and understandably never drawing the appropriate conclusions.[13]

The subsequent direction of utilitarianism may also be responsible for our preconceptions when we read the *Introduction*. J. S. Mill, Henry Sidgwick, G. E. Moore (at least as far as he could be called a utilitarian), and most others seem never to have conceived of any but a universalistic utilitarianism. This might be because they concentrated on certain crucial oppositions: egoism against morality, for example, and hedonism against broader value theories. The only philosopher who seems to have imagined that Bentham might have had a dual standard is Sidgwick, but unfortunately he never identified the evidence that suggested this to him. And even this most acute philosopher was blind to the differences between parochialism and universalism, each of which is manifest in quotations from Bentham that Sidgwick uses when discussing this question.[14]

But, after all these factors have been listed, one should still remain dissatisfied. For the dual standard seems an intuitively implausible position. If it were claimed that Bentham was a parochialist, one might wonder how he could have thought it morally permissible to neglect the interests of those beyond the borders of one's political community. And our doubts must be severely aggravated when we are asked to believe that he held the more complex and apparently less natural position which I have ascribed to him, one that divides the moral life in two.

---

[13] Frederick Copleston, *A History of Philosophy* (Doubleday, N.Y., 1967), vol VIII, pt. I, ch. II, sec. 3; pp. 26ff.
[14] *The Methods of Ethics*, bk. I, note appended to the end of ch. VI.

The answer one must give is that this was not his fundamental position, and it is time we reminded ourselves of this fact. Bentham thought of the dual standard as derivative. The very grounds we have for saying this are the basis for the dual-standard reading itself. We have defended the dual-standard interpretation. Now let us look more closely at Bentham's derivation.

5

THE DEVELOPMENT OF BENTHAM'S POSITION

1. *Some Problems for the Derivation*

IT is essential to my interpretive hypothesis that Bentham's dual standard in the *Introduction* was not his fundamental doctrine but was derivative. Let us review very briefly the origins of this interpretation, and we shall see why this is so.

Bentham's 'explicit and determinate account' of the principle of utility speaks of promoting the happiness of 'the party whose interest is in question', but he fails to specify who that should be. He does immediately go on, however, to explain utility in terms of the happiness of 'the party whose interest is considered', who, he says, might be either 'the community in general' or 'a particular individual' (*IPML*, I, 2–3). Later in the book he defines ethics as 'the art of directing men's actions to the production of the greatest possible quantity of happiness, on the part of those whose interest is in view'. He then divides this into the art of self-government (or private ethics, which is concerned only with the direction of a single agent's behaviour) and the art of government (which concerns the direction of other human agents) (*IPML*, XVII, 2–4). These divisions, of utility and of ethics, are not equivalent; but it is easy to see how they might correspond. We may suppose that Bentham's basic, underlying conception of the principle of utility is that one should always serve the happiness or interests of those under one's governance. (Government should serve the interests of those governed.) This would explain why Bentham defines and divides ethics in the way he does (in terms of those being directed rather than those affected) and also the dual character of utility. It also enables us to repair the vagueness in his 'explicit and determinate account' of the basic principle.

We have seen how a good deal of this interpretative account can be defended on textual and philosophical grounds. But that takes us only part of the way, for Bentham's derivation of the dual standard from the more basic differential principle of utility is not explicit in the text but only suggested there. The most plausible reconstruction of Bentham's derivation seems open to objections. But many difficulties accruing to the derivation can be dealt with adequately, if not by showing that the implicit argument is sound, then at least by showing that it can be attributed to Bentham anyway. We shall consider the derivation and its difficulties in this chapter.

Before we proceed, a word should be said about the fact that I have placed so much weight on a few terse remarks of Bentham's. My justification is, first of all, that they are definitive statements, not incidental comments. Secondly, Bentham's language seems meant quite literally. For example, the partition of ethics and the dual standard rest upon his claim that one may 'direct' one's own actions or those of other agents, and 'direct' here does not seem intended as a loose way of speaking. I have suggested that 'self-direction' (which would come under the art of self-government) concerns what one may be said to do of his own accord, and we have since had reason to qualify this only by excepting official actions. The idea of 'directing' other agents seems straightforward too. A government may be thought to 'direct', or govern, all the members of the political community, and something like this is no doubt Bentham's view.

It should be noted that the words that Bentham uses ('influence' as well as 'direction') and others that we have added (such as 'control') seem well suited to his views about the character of law. A government uses law to provide directives to all who come within its competence; it also involves positive influence and, indeed, control. For he believes that the law must provide motivation for compliance, and he is convinced that this must be done by threatening punishment for disobedience. Governing therefore does not merely involve the establishment of behavioural standards, the announcement of what people are expected to do, while hoping for obedience. Governing involves positive direction, influence, and even control.

This can be exaggerated, and Bentham's attitudes towards the use of punishment are sometimes misconstrued. Critics can lead one to imagine the utilitarian approving capital punishment or gruesome tortures as penalties for overtime parking, for only such sanctions might be effective against a practice that is so difficult to eliminate. But this is absurd. A utilitarian can never allow the cure to be worse than the disease (measuring both by their 'mischief'). Punishments are not supposed to be used except in support of useful or beneficial laws, and even then they should be used only if they are needed, efficacious, and 'profitable'. The utilitarian is not committed to deterring individuals from mischievous behaviour at any cost. Nor, indeed, is he committed to a 'deterrence theory' of punishment, which says that it should be used primarily to discourage people from doing things rather than for 'reforming' them or giving them their 'just deserts'. Bentham subscribes to a deterrence theory in the sense that he believes as a matter of fact that this is the main way in which punishment can usefully be put to work—when it can be justified at all. It is quite clear that he means (and that any consistent utilitarian should mean) that punishment may be used only where and as utility allows.

Even with these necessary qualifications about the way he is prepared to prescribe punishment under law, there is no doubt that he views government as exercising control of an appreciable kind over its subjects. Bentham is not speaking very loosely when he speaks of governments or government functionaries 'directing' other persons' behaviour.

These remarks do not secure the derivation of Bentham's dual standard from the differential principle, however; they only make that topic worth pursuing further. Let us look into some of the problems that arise for the derivation. These mainly concern how he can get from the principle, that one ought to promote the interests of those whose behaviour he is 'directing', to the political standard, or the claim that one who is engaged in political affairs should promote the happiness of all the members of his community.

A number of minor problems, or apparent problems, can be dealt with quickly. For example, since actual lawmakers of politically independent communities are presumably members of the communities they help to govern, they fall within the scope of their own laws; and since the political standard

requires that the interests of all members of the community
be served, for the purpose of its derivation we must regard
lawmakers as 'directing' themselves. But we should be willing
to accept this idea, for it amounts to legislators laying down
rules and providing sanctions for non-compliance, which
might be applied to themselves. We might think we perceive
a difficulty here if we think of lawmakers as having all the
special properties of Bentham's so-called 'sovereign', and consequently imagine that they must be thought of as issuing
commands to themselves. But ordinary government functionaries such as legislators are not the same as that personified
corporate individual, the sovereign, so even if laws are regarded by Bentham as commands and ordinary legislators
must be taken as 'directing' themselves as well as others, it
would not follow that legislators are supposed to be commanding themselves.

A minor qualification of the basic principle is required by
the fact that government does not actually 'direct' those under
its laws in a sense that implies continuous active control. Even
the most oppressive governments are not always ordering one
about. And, while governmental directives are more like
standing orders than simple commands, and thus have continuing force, they do not cover every aspect of behaviour. So
it would seem better to say that those within the scope of the
laws are always *subject to* the government's direction, influence, and control. Bentham's differential principle may be
understood accordingly: one ought to promote the happiness
of those who are *subject to* one's direction, influence, or control—in other words, those under one's governance. This
seems an acceptable qualification, and it has in fact already
been incorporated in some of our formulations.

Some problems concern what might be called borderline
cases and how Bentham can be presumed to deal with them. He
never defines the exact limits of community membership, for
example. Now, residents as well as official citizens must presumably be counted, since they fall under the laws of the community. But what about potential immigrants, including
those who are turned away at the borders or arrested for illeg-
ally crossing them? According to the parochial standard, their
interests need *not* be considered, for they presumably do not

count as members of the community in question; but they fall
within the scope of some of its laws and so they can be regarded
as under that government's 'direction' at least to some degree,
which means that, on the differential principle, their interests
should be served. But I think it can be granted that this is a
special case, a detail that Bentham might well have overlooked,
and that any damage done to the derivation by this complication is in principle reparable. I shall later suggest how
Bentham could have overlooked so many such details. It will
also emerge that Bentham most likely considered his political
standard as applying only to domestic or internal matters,
under which such problems might not be classified.

A more difficult complication arises from the fact that some
laws are regarded by Bentham not as directives to the community at large but for certain public officials in particular. An
important example is that of 'punitory' laws which tell judges
how to deal with convicted offenders (*IPML*, Concluding Note,
6–9). If we were to suppose that those to whom the rules are
directed are those who count, for the purposes of the derivation, as being subject to the relevant sort of direction, influence, and control, then the differential principle would seem
to imply that these laws should serve the interests of the judges.
But we can infer from Bentham's attitudes towards judges that
he would never accept this conclusion. It also conflicts with his
political standard, which presumably applies to punitory rules
as much as to any others and requires serving the interests of
the community as a whole.

Two points can be made. First, Bentham also indicates that
the punitory law strictly implies the ordniary law, and thus
implies a directive to the community at large. Secondly, and
more generally, one might also claim that the class of persons
who count as being *subject to* the government's direction, influence, and control is always the entire community, even when
the government sees fit to lay down directives only to some part
of the community. Even when the government *actively* directs
only some persons by addressing laws in effect to them, it is
exercising its control over the entire community, and therefore
all citizens' interests must, on the differential principle, be
considered. The government's decision to regulate the behaviour of only part of the community in a certain respect

should always be determined on the basis of the interests of the community at large.

Another, possibly more serious, difficulty concerns the lingering question of how 'public ethics' should be defined. In Chapter 3 we noted that Bentham's reference in the *Chrestomathia* to a distinction between 'state-regarding' and 'non-state-regarding ethics' could be taken as implying a division of ethics into mutually exclusive sectors. This enabled us to say that the two parts of the dual standard could not possibly conflict even if personal and community interests happened to diverge. But we also understood that division in terms of the official behaviour of government functionaries, on the one hand, and private behaviour on the other. There are at least two difficulties with this suggestion, however. One, to be dealt with below, arises from the fact that public ethics must cover not merely the official behaviour of government functionaries, but also—and indeed pre-eminently—acts that can be ascribed to the government as a whole, which Bentham calls 'measures of government'. The other problem, on which we shall comment briefly here, concerns the exclusion from public ethics, as it has so far been construed, of the *political* behaviour of *private* individuals—unofficial political action. One might suppose that Bentham would have wanted the political standard of community interest to apply not only to official behaviour but also to political action of every kind. One cannot be certain of this, for when he wrote the *Constitutional Code* (admittedly, much later on), he suggested that he as an individual citizen was propounding the criterion of community interest as the proper standard for government because it made him happy to engage in the hard work of doing so (Bowring, IX, 7). From this one might infer that the political standard does not establish *requirements* for private individuals, even when they are engaged in what we might call political (though unofficial) action. But, whatever Bentham's views at the time of the *Introduction* might have been, the chief difficulties that these considerations pose for the derivation itself are not extremely serious. It seems best to suppose that private and public ethics are mutually exclusive, as we have assumed. The question is how to draw the line between them. The attractiveness of dividing ethics in terms of official versus private behaviour lay in the greater likelihood of developing a sharp boundary between the two sectors, for both theoretical and practical purposes. But other ways of drawing the line, while more complex, are still possible. We can leave the matter there.

The most serious problem concerns a different aspect of the question, what the political standard governs. We have assumed that Bentham's public ethics concerns every official act of a government functionary. But, given the political standard of community interest plus my differential interpretation of Bentham's basic principle, this assumption creates difficulties when we add a fact of which Bentham could not have failed to be aware, namely, that not all members of a political community are actually subject to the control of each public official. In both law and fact, the power and authority of public officials is often limited to certain classes of persons. A military officer is generally empowered to give orders only to his subordinates and not to citizens in general. The specific jurisdiction of a court delimits the class of persons that a given judge is empowered to direct. Administrators generally have very restricted concerns. Now, if Bentham held that one ought to serve those under one's governance, then the class of persons whose interests such public officials should be expected to serve would be much narrower than the entire community. But the political standard, which presumably covers all the official acts of such functionaries, will not allow this, for it requires them always to serve the entire community. This suggests that a standard of community interest which is applicable to all official actions cannot be generated from the differential principle—not in virtue of borderline cases and details that might understandably have been overlooked, but because of certain plain, incontrovertible facts that *must* have been known to Bentham. The difficulty seems obvious enough to discredit my account of Bentham's principle.

It will do no good at this point to employ Bentham's assumption that interests harmonize in order to show that in promoting the interests of any class of persons within the community a public official could be expected to serve the interests of the community at large. For this would only show that the differential principle is to that extent compatible with the political standard of community interest; it would not show how Bentham could believe that the standard of community interest *ought to be applied* in all political affairs. It would not help the derivation.

The most likely explanation is more interesting. We can reconstruct a more elaborate implicit argument that might plausibly be claimed to express Bentham's unarticulated thoughts. The argument has two stages, one dealing with the government as a whole, the second drawing conclusions about the ordinary official conduct of government functionaries. But first some groundwork must be laid.

2. The Government as a Corporate Individual

The argument that I shall reconstruct makes essential use of the idea that a government can be regarded as an individual to whom acts can be ascribed. I mention this now because I wish to forestall misapprehensions. This personification of the government—treating it as if it were a person who can decide as well as act and even exercise control over other persons—this is no better than a fiction, one might argue, and it is incredible to think of Bentham using the notion of a government in such a way. For he warns us of 'linguistic fictions' and 'fictitious entities'. He even turns aside from a most important passage at the beginning of the *Introduction* in order to disabuse us of any fiction that might be suggested by 'the happiness of the community'.

There are two ways of answering this. The first is to show that the idea of government as a corporate individual is compatible with Bentham's strictures about linguistic fictions; the second is to show that Bentham accepted just such 'fictions'. (These answers are complementary, not incompatible.)

Bentham's theory of fictions[1] seems to assume that all nouns and substantive expressions refer to entities, either 'real' or 'fictitious'. Real entities are supposed to be objects of perception, including sensations and ordinary physical objects; fictitious entities are those that are not possible objects of sensation. (Fictitious entities must be distinguished from 'fabulous' ones, which could be perceived if they existed but simply do not exist.) Fictions are therefore numerous in everyday discourse, practically unavoidable in any complex language,

[1] See *Bentham's Theory of Fictions*, ed. C. K. Ogden.

and ubiquitous in technical discourse as in the law. Even to say
'the ball is in motion' is to conjure up such a fiction, according
to Bentham, for one who says it is supposed to be saying literally that the ball is *in* some *thing*, namely motion, while
motion is not a real entity. As this example shows, however,
to conjure up fictions is not to speak nonsense or even to say
something false. (At least, this is Bentham's down-to-earth attitude. He is not inclined to deny the reality of motion.) Statements that imply the existence of fictitious entities are
acceptable if they are thoroughly analysable into statements
about real entities. The latter explain the sense of the former,
and the former can be regarded as true when the latter are
true. Thus, 'the ball is in motion' is not objectionable, because
it is equivalent to 'the ball moves', which implies no fictitious
entities. Both are true when and only when the ball moves. The
trouble with 'the ball is in motion' is simply that it has *misleading* metaphysical implications, about the real existence of
non-perceptible entities, which Bentham as an empiricist will
not allow.

Once we understand the way linguistic fictions operate and
recognize the fictitious character of the implications of certain
expressions, Bentham has no objection to our using these terms.
Thus, once he explains what can sensibly be meant by 'the
happiness of the community', he uses that sort of expression
repeatedly without further comment or qualification. And he
clearly supposes that corresponding statements are true. In a
similar way, he holds, for example, that rights are fictitious
entities.[2] There is no such *thing* as *a* right, for no real entity is
denoted by that word. But we can translate the claim that
someone *has* a right into a statement about the actual states
and modifications of real existing things. Intelligible statements about rights are to be understood as statements about

___

[2] *Introduction*, XVI, 2, note e2. In calling rights 'fictitious entities', Bentham
is not rejecting them, or the idea of them, for ascriptions of rights can be given
truth-conditions, and some such claims are true even if others are false. This
idea should therefore not be confused with his rejection of the very idea of so-
called 'natural rights'. '*Natural rights* is simple nonsense: natural and im-
prescriptable rights, rhetorical nonsense, – nonsense upon stilts' (*Anarchical
Fallacies*, in Bowring, II, 501). The point of this passage is to contrast these
'pretended' rights with straightforward legal rights, with which Bentham is
afraid they may be confused.

others' useful or beneficial obligations, and these are analysable in turn by reference to directives and the threat of punishment. So we may talk about rights too. There is consequently
no reason for Bentham to refrain from speaking of the government *as if it were* a single individual, which deliberates, decides, acts, and so on, provided that he believes such statements
to be strictly analysable in terms of real individuals. Bentham
obviously had such beliefs.

We shall later see how, in developing his theory of law, Bentham unself-consciously makes continuous use of the notion of
a 'sovereign', He employs this term as if it referred in any
political community to one single human being, who is the
centre and source of all political power. But Bentham is quite
clear that there need not be, and that there generally is not,
one such person. Power is distributed among actual persons in
highly complex ways, and much of it is exercised jointly by
groups of individuals such as those who make up legislatures.
But it is sometimes useful to think, or to speak, as if the political power in a state were concentrated in a single individual,
and Bentham does so throughout *Of Laws in General*. This
notion of a sovereign is very similar to, if not the same as, the
notion of government as a corporate individual. It should be
observed that, in the section of the *Introduction* that concerns
us here, Bentham uses the term 'legislator' in a similar way, not
referring to any particular legislator but rather to the collective
legislative power in a community, as if it were all gathered in
one person (*IPML*, XVII, i). This way of speaking is quite
natural. And so is Bentham's suggestion that a government can
be regarded as a corporate individual.

3. *The Implicit Derivation*

The argument can now be reconstructed as follows. If Bentham has the differential principle I have imputed to him,
then the only way in which it might be thought to generate
the political standard of community interest is by virtue of the
government's *collective* control over the entire political community. And if one is prepared to talk about 'the government'
as if it were an individual person, then one is free to reason in
this way. As a whole, the government possesses and exercises
the power to determine what each member of the community

shall do. Given the differential principle, it follows that the government should serve the interests of the entire community; it should serve the interests of each of its subjects in every one of its actions, that is, in everything it can be said to do. For all of the members of the community are subject to its direction, influence, and control. (As we have seen, the sense in which this can be regarded as true is unaffected by the fact that the government may sometimes restrict its attention to a particular part of the community. For even if its immediate concerns are limited and local, its continuing competence is not. This point might perhaps be qualified to take account of constitutional limitations).

But the argument must have a second stage, for so far it says nothing at all about the ordinary acts of real individuals. The collective power of the government as a whole is not transmitted undiluted to each public official. Suppose we allow that the government as a whole ought to serve the interests of all its subjects, in everything it does. What relevance does this have to the everyday conduct of government functionaries?

The obvious and impeccable but trivial answer is, that each public official always ought to do what would most contribute to *the government's* serving the interests of the several members of the community. This is not helpful, however, because it is not clear what else can be said, in general terms, about such conduct. Should public officials always try to serve the general happiness? Should they test each and every one of their official acts by direct application of the community interest standard? That does not seem to follow, so a political standard which is applicable to the official behaviour of government functionaries is not yet forthcoming. Can an argument bridge this gap?

A satisfactory argument may seem impossible. It is fashionable nowadays to claim that if everyone in a community actually *tried* to serve the general happiness, then the opposite would result; that adherence to useful rules would be far more likely to serve the desired end; and that this is particularly true within complex organizations which have a division of labour, such as governments. It may be argued, therefore, that Bentham should want to establish rules that public officials are to follow; that these rules should be selected on the basis that, if followed, they are most likely to promote the general happiness; and that public officials should *not* apply the community interest standard directly to their behaviour. But Bentham seems to want public officials to apply the standard directly to each and every action they perform in the conduct of their offices. How could he think that this would serve the general interest?

It should be observed, however, that Bentham is committed to the programme of laying down rules to govern the conduct of public officials. This is quite clear from his writings on government. The rules could be divided roughly into two groups—those that determine the structure of government and those that concern the conduct of officials within the predetermined structure. Some rules would divide and distribute official functions, for example, and these would allow varying degrees of official discretion; other rules would serve as guides for officials to use in reaching specific decisions within their areas of discretion. Beyond a certain point, officials would presumably be advised to apply the political standard of community interest directly.

The question that remains, therefore, is whether Bentham can be regarded as holding that such rules ought to be followed. For he might agree that the general interest is best served by having government run along the lines laid down by such rules; but he also wants the standard of community interest to apply to each and every official action. Can the two positions be made compatible? Only if Bentham believes that in each and every case the general interest is most likely to be served when public officials abide by the rules as far as they extend. That is, Bentham must be committed to the assumption that whenever a public official applies the standard of community interest *directly* to his conduct, he should conclude that it is most likely that the community will best be served by his adhering to rules that are grounded in utility. And it seems reasonable to suppose that Bentham believed this (*even if* he recognized the *possibility*, discussed in Chapter 3, that the general interest could sometimes best be served by departing from the rules). It is the sort of distributive assumption that Bentham was prone to make. (See e.g. *IPML*, XII, 17.)

In other words, it would seem that, if Bentham can be said

to begin his derivation of the political standard by requiring
that the *government* serve the community interest in everything it does, then he is likely to complete it by saying that the
best or perhaps the only way of guaranteeing this end is by set-
ting the same goal for *each government functionary* in the ordinary conduct of his office. We can help him to achieve this
end by laying down maximally useful rules for him to follow
(outside the scope of which he is free to apply the community
interest standard directly). He is always more likely to serve the
community's interest, Bentham believes, if he follows these
rules than if he diverges from them.

There are difficulties with such an argument, of course, as
we have already noted. But our question is whether it can be
imputed to Bentham. It must be admitted that by now we have
gone well beyond the text on which the derivation is supposedly based. My claim is not that the foregoing is strictly determined by that text; only that it is compatible with the text
and helps us to make more sense of what Bentham may have
had in mind.

In Chapter 4 I mentioned the possibility that Bentham
distinguished between political acts in general (the subject of
IPML, I, 6) and measures of government (the subject of *IPML*,
I, 7). We can now see how this fits into the reconstruction of
Bentham's derivation. The ordinary official conduct of government functionaries constitutes the first class of 'actions', while
the second corresponds to the things that can be said to be
done by a government as a whole. This suggestion is not
threatened by the fact that Bentham explains 'measures of
government' as 'but a particular kind of action, performed by
a particular person or persons' (*IPML*, I, 7). There are two
possible ways in which this explanation can now be understood. First, the 'person' referred to might be the government
as a whole. Second (and more likely), the person or persons
could be those in virtue of whose behaviour the government
can have actions ascribed to it. For Bentham unquestionably
would hold that whatever a government can intelligibly be
said to do must be analysable in terms of the conduct of ordinary persons, sometimes one person, sometimes more than
one. He need not hold that what a government does is simply
identical with what an individual human agent does; the rela-

tionship can be more complex. There are perhaps cases in which an official act of a single human being can amount to an act of the government as a whole (as when a monarch, president, or prime minister does certain things). In such cases the single act would be a member of each class, though possibly under different descriptions. As something done by a government functionary in his official capacity it would count as an ordinary political act, while as something attributable to the government as a whole it would count as a measure of government. More commonly, however, measures of government would be analysable in terms of a variety of things done by a number of ordinary individuals. This can be illustrated in the cases of actions attributable to a legislative body as a whole: these result from a variety of acts—including several acts of voting—of a number of individuals. Even if we make the overly simple assumption that what a legislature does is attributable to the government as a whole, and thus counts as a measure of government, we must still distinguish between that kind of 'act' and the acts of the several legislators. Now, Bentham may well have underestimated the complexity of the relationship between these two kinds of actions. But, whether he did or not, he would still have been prepared to make such a distinction, it would fit nicely into the two stages of his derivation, and it would incidentally suggest a way of sorting out Chapter I of the *Introduction*.

4. *Critique of the Derivation*

Although the foregoing account is the simplest reconstruction of the passages in question, difficulties still accrue to it. The chief one must be that a differential principle like the one I have sketched would not lead to Bentham's *dual* standard. It would seem to yield a variety of standards, depending on the circumstances.

As I have imagined it, Bentham's basic principle says that one ought to serve the interests of those who are subject to one's 'direction'. This fits both his 'explicit and determinate account' and his division of ethics. But the division of ethics as we have construed it seems excessively narrow, for it allows only two of many possible types of interpersonal 'direction'. It recognizes control over an entire community, directly by a government and indirectly by its functionaries, which yields the political standard of community interest. And it acknowledges the existence of self-direction, whereby one determines how he himself, alone, shall behave, which yields the self-interest standard for private ethics. But it does not seem to envisage other kinds of influence over other persons. And yet personal influence outside government can be very wide and in any case effective enough to warrant comparison with the influence that government enjoys over its subjects. In such cases, and to the degree that such influence is exercised, one would expect Bentham's position to be that one ought to serve the interests of those subject to one's 'direction'. If he *has* the differential principle, then he *should* say, not merely that one ought to serve either the interests of the entire community or else one's own but also that sometimes one ought to serve the interests of other individuals (or groups of individuals), that is, those who happen to be subject to one's personal direction, influence, or control.

In all this we have assumed that Bentham's use of the term 'government' in 'the art of government' refers to government in the ordinary political sense. This is somewhat awkward, since 'government' in 'the art of *self*-government' would then presumably have a slightly different sense. There were some grounds for this reading. Apart from his reference in the *Chrestomathia* to 'state-regarding ethics', these include his apparently *political* standard of community interest and his division of the art of government into the subordinate arts of 'legislation' and 'administration', the title and his treatment of which suggest the ordinary political senses of those terms.

But it is possible that Bentham meant 'the art of government' to be interpreted somewhat more loosely, so that it could cover all cases in which interpersonal influence is exerted. This would fit his 'art of education', the discussion of which follows that of the art of government. Bentham treats it as a branch of the art of government, 'in as far as it concerns the direction of persons in a non-adult state' (*IPML*, XVII, 5). Unfortunately, he does not clearly say whose interests the exercise of such an art is supposed to serve (although it would not be unreasonable to assume that it should serve those being educated, which would fit the differential principle). (See *IPML*, XVI, 4–6.)

If Bentham meant 'the art of government' to encompass *all* cases of interpersonal direction, influence, and control, then we would have to understand the division of ethics and the dual standard somewhat differently than we have done so far. The dual standard would represent only two of the main implications of his basic principle. Bentham could perhaps be understood to say that when one acts in an official governmental capacity one ought to serve the interests of the entire community; when one acts 'privately', one ought to serve oneself; otherwise, one ought to serve the interests of those who are subject to one's direction, influence, or control, such as the non-adults one is responsible for 'educating'. This would mean, however, that Bentham's clear summary at the end of Section i of the final chapter (*IPML*, XVII, 20) must be regarded as an incomplete statement of the standards that he thought were subordinate to his utilitarianism, snice it covers only the two standards of community and self-interest (and gives no intimation of any others).

In this context, we should take brief note of Bentham's lengthy discussion of institutional forms in which a private person is legally empowered to exercise control over another (*IPML*, XVI, 40–55). To some extent, at least, the *point* of such relationships is to serve the interests of the person doing the controlling, rather than the person being controlled, and this might seem to cause some difficulty for the differential interpretation. It is true that Bentham discusses so-called 'fiduciary' relations, such as that of a guardian to his ward, whom the guardian is supposed to serve. But he also discusses 'beneficial' relations, such as that of a master to his servant, whom the master is expected to employ to his own advantage. If Bentham thought that 'beneficial' relations could be justified on the ground of utility, it might seem as if his basic principle did not require that we always serve the interests of those subject to our direction, influence, or control.

The lessons to be learned from these discussions are not nearly so clear, however. When Bentham discusses various legal relations, he sometimes does argue that some would be endorsed by utility (e.g., at *IPML*, XVI, 40, note x3) but he

does not always talk this way. And the general discussion in
the *Introduction* could easily be taken as a survey of possible
institutional forms that *might* be made enforceable by law,
chiefly for the purpose of showing how various types of 'mischief' can arise from breaches of established relationships (cf.
e.g., *IPML*, XVI, 27, note m2; 42; 46). This would harmonize
with the conception and design of Chapter XVI. If so, a discussion of the mischief that could arise from violations of the rules
governing master-servant relations would not by itself imply
that Bentham gives a utilitarian endorsement to that type of
relation. But even if he thought that such relations can be
justified on the grounds of their utility, he might be taken as
reasoning that under certain circumstances their legal establishment would serve the best interests of potential servants
(*IPML*, XVI, 43).

The question is a complicated one. We must distinguish, for
example, between the initial governmental decision to allow
and enforce such relations and the master's attitude towards
his servant. The government's decision is presumably governed
by the political standard of community interest. But what
standard applies to the master's actions towards his servant?
On the basis of a direct application of the differential principle
we should say that the master ought to serve the interests of the
servant. On the basis of the original dual standard, we would
have said that he should serve himself—which is what the institution envisages. But according to Bentham's view in *Of
Laws in General,* the master's legally enforceable instructions
to his servant must count as legal 'mandates', on a par with
legal rules and commands issued directly by the sovereign, and
they should then presumably serve the interests of the community. Bentham's position is unclear. But it should also be
observed that, however we resolve the matter, some such difficulties will accrue to the competing interpretations of Bentham's utilitarianism, for on each of them we would expect
Bentham to say that the master ought to employ his servant, not
to serve his own interests, but to serve the interests of all
affected or the interests of the entire community.

These considerations suggest, therefore, not so much conclusive evidence against the differential interpretation of Bentham's principle as serious gaps in Bentham's development of

his own position. Many aspects of the overall view that seems implicit in the *Introduction* are left unclear. Although the derivation that I have reconstructed is not closely determined by the text, I am inclined to believe that it captures Bentham's intent as well as can be done, even if the gaps in the resultant position turn out to be quite serious. For we have very strong evidence that he held the two standards and that they turn upon the definition and division of ethics. It also seems most plausible to suppose that these assume a more basic principle of utility, such as the one I have sketched.

How could Bentham have been so careless and vague? Perhaps through a combination of satisfaction and distraction. In writing the *Fragment on Government* several years before completing the *Introduction,* he had endorsed a 'principle of utility'. But that seems to have been an early stage in the development of his thought. The idea of a 'greatest happiness principle' was not original, and it seems to have been current at the time. His concern in the *Fragment* was entirely with government, so it was not necessary for him then to have decided whether he endorsed the standard of community interest for all matters of ethics as well as government, or thought a different standard applies to 'private ethics'. It is not implausible to suppose that, while writing the *Introduction* later, Bentham thought he had discovered a powerful 'utilitarian' principle which could yield not only the community interest standard for judging the affairs of government but the principle of prudence as a bonus. How tempting such a principle and derivation would have been! But just at that time his attention was drawn away from his inadequately developed derivation and he failed to give it the critical examination it required. In writing the final chapter of the *Introducton,* he was at first preoccupied with the very different topics that he had intended to cover in it (such as the distinction between civil and penal law). Later he was distracted by and then became immersed in much more general questions about laws 'in general'. His continued research delayed final completion of the book, persuaded him to postpone its publication even after it had almost all been printed, and drove him to devote a year or two to developing what was to be his fullest discussion of the nature of law. When he finally published the book he

did not return to his discussion of ethics. We should also re-
member that Bentham could not yet have been sensitive to
many problems associated with his differential principle or
with its dual (or multiple) standards. For he did not yet recognize how interests can really conflict; that came only much
later. And so, we find in the first and last chapters of the *Introduction* the limits of Bentham's moral reflections for many
years to come. His work on law and government led him this
far into the principles of morals, but it seems to have led him
no further.

5. *The Defence of an Axiom*

One might expect to get further insight into Bentham's conception of the principle of utility by examining his arguments
for it. But he declares that a 'direct proof' of the principle is
impossible (*IPML*, I, 11; thus foreshadowing J. S. Mill's contention in his essay on *Utilitarianism*). His explanation can
be understood in more than one way, but it suggests the now
generally accepted view that a principle which is supposed to
be the most general and comprehensive standard for evaluation cannot be derived from any other. The natural question
that arises is whether an 'indirect' proof is possible—whether
any argument could conceivably be given to show that it is
irrational to reject or most rational to embrace such a principle. (Mill presented an argument, despite his disclaimer
about direct proofs.) Bentham makes some suggestions along
these lines, in Chapters I and II of the *Introduction*, though
his arguments seem designed to show that the principle sur-
vives by default, in virtue of the unacceptability of alternative
principles. These arguments are weak, partly because the alternatives are crudely drawn, as either the 'principle of asceti-
cism' (which holds that happiness should be minimized rather
than maximized) or the 'principle of sympathy and antipathy',
otherwise called the 'principle of caprice', apparently meant
to cover *all* the remaining possibilities, which are alleged
merely to express arbitrary sentiments or attitudes. These passages lend credence to Mill's contention that Bentham did not
trouble himelf with the underpinnings of his utilitarianism
and was unable sympathetically to comprehend the different
views of others.

THE DEVELOPMENT OF BENTHAM'S POSITION

Bentham does offer some positive suggestions, however. He sometimes seems to say that the principle is implicit in all our reasonings, but he usually claims much less, allowing, as he wishes to do, for the existence of moral 'prejudices'. A more systematic attempt to defend his principle could be reconstructed out of some of his suggestions, although the upshot is inconclusive and also too vague to provide a more precise characterization of his principle. He maintains, for example, that a basic principle for morals and legislation should have universal application and should leave no room for the legitimate use of different principles. (He is unclear, however, whether this is required by the very nature of evaluation or is simply needed for practical purposes if we are to settle moral and political disputes.) He insists that we must have an objective standard—one that can be used to assess and to correct attitudes, sentiments, and moral impulses, rather than merely to express them. (But there is also some reason to suppose that Bentham conceived of his own principle as expressing a certain sentiment, and it is not clear how his principle would be different from any other in this regard.) He argues that an acceptable principle of conduct must make use of empirical tests (but he invalidly assumes that these must concern the contingent effects of acts and cannot concern the acts themselves, apart from their effects). He then assumes that the only relevant effects are those that concern the happiness and welfare of persons. He thus seems to beg all the important questions.

Can anything be gleaned from his discussion that might be useful for our purposes? In view of echoes found in other works, one might mention his suggestion that an alternative principle to that of utility would be found to be 'despotical, and hostile to all the rest of human race' (*IPML*, I, 14). This seems to anticipate a comment he was to make much later, at the start of the *Constitutional Code* :

> In saying, as above, the proper end of government is the greatest happiness of all, or, in case of competition, the greatest happiness of the greatest number, it seems to me that I have made a declaration of peace and good will to all men.
>
> On the other hand, were I to say, the proper end of government is the greatest happiness of some one, naming him, or of some few, naming them, it seems to me that I should be making a declaration

of war against all men, with the exception of that one, or of those few. (Bowring, IX, 5)

But this could be construed as an argument for either a differential principle (such as the one I have imputed to Bentham) or a universalistic one. As the context makes clear, however, he uses this argument in support of a *parochial* standard for government. So these suggestions do not really help us to determine the precise nature of his principle or to understand why he chose one rather than other possible forms of utilitarianism.

A different though somewhat related suggestion is made in Essay I of the *Principles of International Law* (which was, however, constructed after Bentham's death from manuscripts said to be dated between 1786 and 1789; if faithful to those manuscripts it should reflect his thoughts some time after the *Introduction* was written). There he says:

The end of conduct which a sovereign ought to observe relative to his own subjects,—the end of the internal laws of a society,— ought to be the greatest happiness of the society concerned. This is the end which individuals will unite in approving, if they approve of any. (Bowring, II, 537)

The suggestion is that the validity of the relevant standard is shown by the fact that everyone would approve of it, if they could all approve of one single standard.[3] But, once again, this test does not clearly lead us to one of the competing interpretations; once again, Bentham uses it to argue for the parochial political standard.

This essay does bring out other interesting aspects of his position at that time which are relevant to our inquiry. His question in the essay is how one nation should behave with respect to others: it concerns international rather than domestic affairs. He asks whether the sovereign of a state should use the same standard of his community's happiness in external matters, as he ought to do internally, or whether he should aim instead at 'the common and equal utility of all nations' (Bowring, II, 537). Bentham argues for the second alternative, and thus takes the side of internationalism instead

---

[3] The intriguing contractarian suggestions of this passage seem never to have been developed further by Bentham.

of the simple pursuit of national interest. He thus avoids the charge of moral chauvinism, which seemed to be invited by his unqualified acceptance of the parochial standard for political affairs. It now appears that the parochial standard was intended only for application to the internal affairs of societies and to have no direct implications outside that context. (That it has indirect implications is part of the point of the essay.) We cannot of course be sure that this was Bentham's view when he wrote the *Introduction*, but it seems consistent with it, for that book deals only with domestic political matters. And if, as Bentham assumes, political communities are independent, then his differential principle would have no general implications across national boundaries.

These limitations of Bentham's parochial standard are significant and revealing, but it should also be emphasized that the essay does not display a universalistic orientation. If such a standpoint were adopted, that would be obvious, for a universalistic principle could be used to show that the relations between societies should be governed by their common utility, since Bentham would view this as equivalent to the common utility of all persons, which universalism demands. But Bentham never suggests any such argument.

The essay can be regarded, rather, as an attempt to show that internationalism is really in each nation's best interest. Thus, in siding with internationalism Bentham does not reject the standard of national interest. But, as we shall see, this does not mean that a basic parochial principle is assumed either. The argument turns upon an analogy between the internal and external affairs of sovereign political states. Bentham treats each independent nation as if it were (or could be represented by) a single individual 'sovereign', and thus he argues that, as the individuals within a society would accept the standard of community interest for domestic politics, so the sovereigns of different societies should accept the corresponding standard among nations. Why would individuals within a society agree to such a standard? The argument seems to be that a sovereign (now viewed as if he were an ordinary individual who does all the governing for his own society) inevitably learns or should learn by experience that he cannot achieve his ends and therefore must be frustrated by the 'resist-

ance' of his subjects to his measures unless he serves their interests along with his own. Governing in the interests of all
who are governed is thus the 'line of least resistance' for him
in domestic political affairs. Bentham then seems to say that
the same considerations apply between states (which are to
one another as different individuals): pursuit of 'the common
and equal utility of all nations' is the 'line of least resistance'
internationally too.

This seems the simplest reconstruction of the text, and one
would advance it most confidently if the resulting argument
were not so weak and inconclusive. For, taken as a sufficient
defence of certain principles of 'international law', the argument rests upon some strong assumptions. Perhaps the most
plausible is that nations and ordinary individuals can always
adjust their interests so as to avoid conflict with the interests
of others and thus avoid frustration, and still have as good a
chance of happiness. It may assume that frustration is assigned
great weight in the relevant calculations (because it ignores the
possibility that some frustration might profitably be accepted
in order to obtain greater satisfactions in the long run). It
assumes that nations and individuals are sufficiently equal and
uncoordinated to rule out complete dominance of some by
others. And it would seem to require an indefinitely long run
in which natural forces can be allowed to do their work. In
this connection, however, Bentham suggests a possible reason
why interests are assumed by him to converge in the long run:
there is supposed to be a natural tendency for individuals to
adjust their interests, aims, and goals in order to minimize
frustration—that is, to take the 'line of least resistance'.

There are two reasons why this might still be taken as
Bentham's argument, even though so weak. It may represent
only one consideration, not all that he thinks can conceivably
be said, in favour of internationalism. And, viewed in this way,
it offers a striking parallel with a passage in the *Introducton*.
As we have seen before, Bentham seems to argue that the so-
called 'duties' of probity and beneficence (towards other persons) are supported by considerations of prudence, in virtue of
our natural sympathies (*IPML*, XVII, 7). Here his argument
turns on national self-interest—or prudence writ large. And
the specific principles of international law that Bentham pro-

poses in this essay, on the basis of his internationalist conclusions, can quite readily be viewed as 'duties' between
nation-states on the pattern of probity and beneficence.

It does not follow, however, that Bentham's basic principle
is parochial, for none of this conflicts with his idea that self-
interest should be the standard for action in 'private' affairs.
The argument could more strongly tempt one to speculate
that Bentham's root idea might be some notion of prudence—
however confusedly he uses it to get the principles he more
clearly espouses. It can also be said that his views about international law do not threaten the differential interpretation of
his basic principle.

TOPIC TWO
BENTHAM ON THE NATURE OF LAW

6

THE IMPERATIONAL THEORY OF LAW

1. *An Apparent Contradiction*

WE turn now to Bentham's conception of a law. We have seen how in the *Introduction* Bentham conceives of government as 'directing' all the members of a political community. He also suggests how important punishment is within a legal system. These two ideas are closely related to Bentham's conception of a law. But what, exactly, is his notion of a law? A close examination of the outgrowth of the *Introduction—Of Laws in General*—suggests new interpretive problems.

It should be emphasized that we are no longer concerned with Bentham's utilitarianism—at least, not directly. We are concerned with Bentham's contributions as a legal theorist—a founder of analytical jurisprudence—who sought to *understand* the law. Let us see where this led him.

There is a natural temptation to think of laws as either commands or prohibitions. Unlike conventional moral standards and some other social rules, laws can be deliberately laid down and changed by specified procedures. It therefore seems reasonable to think of them (unlike other rules) as issuing from or at least adopted by ordinary human lawmakers. Laws also tell us what must or must not be done. No wonder, then, that the 'command' theory of law is a traditional view, shared by philosophers of many different persuasions and moral outlooks.

The modern and most important form of this conception is the imperative theory of law ascribed to the nineteenth-century English jurist, John Austin.[1] Austin believed that the entire

[1] For an exposition and criticism of such an 'Austinian' imperative theory, see H. L. A. Hart, *The Concept of Law* (Clarendon Press, Oxford, 1961), chs.

content of a legal system could be reduced to commands and prohibitions issuing from the 'sovereign' of an independent political state—some person or set of persons whose commands are generally followed and who is not in the habit of obeying others. By threatening punishment for disobedience, the sovereign imposes legal 'obligations' on his subjects. Austin thus regarded individual laws as coercive commands.

Austin was the direct juristic heir of Bentham, and it has generally been thought that Bentham had the same conception of law. As he never espoused that theory explicitly, one might suppose that he anticipated and perhaps paved the way for his successor's more rigorous and developed theory. But *Laws* tells a different story, which may be summarized as follows.

Although Bentham shared some of Austin's basic assumptions, for example that laws are to be viewed as expressions of a sovereign's will, and some of his conclusions, for example that a legal system may be considered a set of coercive commands, he also maintained that *permissive* laws—which say what *may* or *need not* be done, rather than what ought or ought not to be done—can express a sovereign's will. He held that commands and prohibitions (and 'imperatival' rules and utterances generally) are but one species of the genus *imperation*, of which permissive laws and similar rules and utterances constitute another species. Working from the basic assumptions that were later used by the Austinian imperative theory, Bentham thus recognized more types of law as fundamental.

Bentham's view diverges from the narrower imperative theory. It is significantly original, not only because it acknowledges permissive laws within an Austinian framework, but also because it incorporates one of the earliest systems of what we now call 'deontic' logic—the logical principles that govern restrictions and permissions.[2]

II–IV. Hart has also pointed out to me that there is some evidence that Austin entertained views similar to Bentham's on Permissive Law; see Austin's *Lectures on Jurisprudence*, 5th edn., p. 355, for a very brief discussion of permissive laws. I shall not deal with the proper interpretation of Austin's own views here.

[2] Although discussion of the more general 'modal' logic (concerning necessity and probability) goes back at least to Aristotle, systematic treatment of deontic logic in particular is usually traced to G. H. von Wright, 'Deontic Logic', *Mind*, lx (1951), 1–15.

In attempting to reconstruct Bentham's full conception of law, however, one is faced with apparent contradictions. Even in *Of Laws in General*, Bentham suggests that he subscribes to the imperative theory. In arguing that all laws create some 'mischief'—one of his characteristic claims—he seems to assume that all laws are coercive commands. Thus he explicitly accepts but implicitly rejects permissive laws.

The issues involved are central to Bentham's concerns. His attempt to understand the nature of law was chiefly motivated by his overriding interest in social reform, especially reform of the law. He believed, of course, that laws should always be judged by their tendency to promote human happiness or welfare—in short, by their 'utilities'. And he saw that their beneficial consequences had to be weighed against the harm they could cause. It was therefore important for him to ascertain whether laws have *unavoidable* disutilities. His argument that all laws are mischievous, at least to some degree, provided an answer. Bentham also used the argument for polemical purposes—for example, to inveigh against 'natural lawyers' who blindly extol the supposed virtues of English law, acknowledging neither its frequent inhumanity, corruption, and inefficiency, nor the price that must be paid for having even the best of all possible laws.

How should we view the apparent contradictions in Bentham's legal philosophy? One might say that it contains divergent and sometimes incompatible tendencies, a verdict some critics would regard as more generous than just. But *Of Laws in General* inspires greater confidence in Bentham's care and rigour, and the contradiction may well dissolve on closer scrutiny. One possible explanation is that this book, which he never prepared for publication, was written when Bentham's basic theory of law was developing most rapidly. There is evidence that the relevant parts of what is now Chapter X, in which he fully admits permissive laws, were written somewhat later than Chapter VI, in which he argues that laws are mischievous and implies that they are coercive commands.[3] One could imagine that the coercive command theory came first and that Bentham discovered only later, while reworking Chapter X, the full implications of the more basic idea that

[3] See Hart's Introduction to *Laws*, p. xxxix.

laws express a sovereign's will. It is not certain, however, that this appealingly simple solution of the problem can be sustained, for Bentham mentions permissive laws in another chapter that may be of early origin (*OLG*, II, 8–9).[4] And I am unaware of any evidence that he later disavowed the claim that laws are mischievous. One ought, therefore, to explore the possibility that Bentham's imperational theory of law is compatible with some version of the claim that laws are mischievous.

2. *Law as Mischief*

Bentham's full definition of 'a law' indicates that his basic conception of law is similar in many ways to Austin's:

A law may be defined as an assemblage of signs declarative of a volition conceived or adopted by the *sovereign* in a state, concerning the conduct to be observed in a certain *case* by a certain person or persons, who in the case in question are or are supposed to be subject to his power: such volition trusting for its accomplishment to the expectation of certain events which it is intended such declaration should on occasion be a means of bringing to pass, and the prospect of which it is intended should act as a motive upon those whose conduct is in question. (*OLG*, I, 1)

This passage refers explicitly to 'the sovereign in a state', who is later said to be the 'source' of all its laws, at least in the sense of 'adopting' laws actually laid down by subordinate lawmakers. The sovereign is briefly described as 'any person or assemblage of persons to whose will a whole political community are (no matter on what account) supposed to pay obedience'.[5] Although Bentham qualified this notion of a sovereign, the differences are immaterial here and can be ignored (*OLG*, II, 1, notes a, b; 2, note d). If we assume that the sovereign's 'declarations' are imperatival and that the motivation on which he relies for obedience is provided by his punitive sanctions, then we can regard Bentham's definition as stating an imperative theory of law. It can of course be read in other ways, but this particular interpretation is not foreign to its spirit and may be encouraged by other considerations.

---

[4] i.e., *Laws*, ch. II, pars. 8–9.

[5] *Laws*, II, 1; cf. *A Fragment on Government*, ch. I, par. 10; in Bowring, I, 263.

For example, Bentham refers to the motivational element of law as its 'force', and this suggests the use of coercion (*OLG*, I, 1). Moreover, one might expect Bentham's analysis to be less precise than that later developed by Austin. More persuasive still is the way Bentham seems to use the imperative theory. It supports his claim that law, whether good or bad, necessarily involves 'mischief'. Let us examine this argument more closely.

Bentham says in *Laws* that 'there must be some person or persons who are bound or in other words coerced by' any law. His language suggests that any other kind of law is *inconceivable*: 'A law by which nobody is bound, a law by which nobody is coerced, a law by which nobody's liberty is curtailed, all these phrases which come to the same thing would be so many contradictions in terms' (*OLG*, VI, 3). He then argues that 'a condition equally necessary to the existence of a law is, that there should be some person or persons who are exposed at least to suffer by it. This condition is in truth a necessary consequence of the latter' (*OLG*, VI, 4). Bentham thus seems to assume that individual laws are coercive commands.

This obvious reading of the passage is reinforced by the fact that, as long as Bentham's conclusion is not overstated, one can distil a satisfactory argument for it from the passage if we take into account his views about mischief in the *Introduction* (XII, 5). There he explains that the mischief or disutility of an act is not limited to the actual pain or other unpleasant or unwanted conditions which it produces, but also includes both the 'alarm' it causes, that is, the expectation or fear of such effects, which Bentham assumes is always painful or unpleasant, and the 'danger' it creates, which is mere risk of pain. This means that the mischief of a law need not involve actual pain, but only the unpleasant awareness of being exposed to sanctions, or perhaps only some risk that someone will be frustrated. Bentham's claim that law is unavoidably mischievous requires him to show, therefore, only that such a risk is entailed by any law—that, as he says, 'some person or persons . . . are exposed at least to suffer by it'. He claims that each law binds, coerces, and curtails the liberty of at least one person and thereby exposes at least one individual to mischief. It inevitably creates at the minimum some 'danger', the chance, that is, that someone will experience pain, have unpleasant sensations, be frustrated, or suffer some other unwanted condition. Acts that are generally agreeable to perform can be disagreeable under some circumstances, he argues, so there is always the risk that a legal requirement will be unpleasant to satisfy. Even when the required act is otherwise pleasant to perform, 'the idea of coercion intervening may of itself be sufficient to give it an opposite effect'. And the curtailment of liberty is a mischief because it reduces the chance that one will be able to do what he pleases and thus makes it more likely that he will be unable to get something he wants. These considerations, which are supposed to show that law is an 'evil' even if 'a necessary evil' (*OLG*, VI, 4), seem to presuppose that all laws are essentially 'imperative', 'obligative', and 'coercive'.

The trouble, however, is that Bentham also explicitly recognizes laws that are in his words 'unimperative,' 'unobligative', and 'uncoercive' (*OLG*, X, ii, 6).

3. *Bentham's Two Basic Species of Law*

The imperative theorist recognizes only two types of law, commands and prohibitions. Bentham calls such laws 'imperative', but he does not insist that they be expressed in the imperative mood (*OLG*, X, ii, 6; X, iii, 7; XIII, 4; Appendix D7). To contrast them with permissive laws, and leave open whether they are essentially 'coercive' or 'obligative', I shall call them *restrictive*. Included in the class of restrictive laws are those that might be understood as telling us what must or ought to be done, what is required or forbidden, what is wrong to do or to fail to do, and so on. For convenience, we can follow Bentham's usage and call positive restrictions 'commands' and negative ones 'prohibitions', with the understanding that we are not committing ourselves to an 'imperatival' analysis of laws.

One of the ways in which Bentham was led to acknowledge permissive laws may be reconstructed as follows. By relating permissive and restrictive laws in ways suggested by the attitudes they respectively express, he found it possible to describe logical principles applicable to laws. (But laws are only one family of imperations, that is, those attributable to a sovereign, and so in discovering these logical principles he constructed, in effect, a more general logic of imperation.) He began with the idea that laws are expressions of a sovereign's will, but in considering the attitudes expressed by restrictive laws he observed that their absence is theoretically possible: the absence of restrictive attitudes could be expressed in permissive laws. Permissive laws are thus just as real or just as possible as commands and prohibitions. Consequently, Bentham concluded that there are four rather than two elementary types of law, and that they fall into two species, restrictive and permissive. Bentham was clearly no simple imperativist. He could not maintain that all laws must be coercive commands, because some laws, he held, are not command-like at all.

I turn now to some details of this imperational theory of law. A law is supposed to express certain attitudes of the lawmaker towards the performance of a given act. Let us say for now that a command expresses his desire to see a certain act performed, while a prohibition expresses the desire to see an act omitted. Thus 'Do A' and 'Do not do A' express what might be called 'contrary attitudes' on the part of the sovereign towards the performance of act A. Nevertheless, Bentham realized that positive and negative forms of imperation are interchangeable. 'The law which prohibits the mother from starving her child commands her to take care that it be fed. The one may be at pleasure translated or *converted* into the other' (*OLG*, X, ii, 5). It may be awkward or difficult to construct completely accurate conversions, but they are always possible in principle. The command of an act can be regarded as the prohibition of its omission, and vice versa.[6]

Bentham's claim seems sound. Although it often makes a difference for linguistic convenience or other practical purposes, whether we use affirmative or negative forms in formulating restrictions seems immaterial from a purely logical standpoint. The substance of what is said can be expressed either way. This is so even if we use the imperative mood. 'Do A' can always be stated, 'Do not fail to do A', thus changing a command into a prohibition. Prohibitions can similarly be

6 Bentham realized that the possibility of specifying behaviour in alternative ways was independent of a real, extra-linguistic distinction between acts and omissions; see *Introduction*, VII, 8–10.

converted into commands.[7] Similar conversions are also possible between the two types of permission.

Imperational conversion has an interesting theoretical consequence which was not expressly noted by Bentham. Since
either form of restrictive law may be defined in terms of the
other, the conceptual assumptions or the basic linguistic ap-
paratus of, say, an imperative theory of law would need to
include only one of the two restrictive forms. Since permissive
laws are also convertible, an imperational theory of law, such
as Bentham's, in fact need recognize only two basic species of
imperation—restrictive and permissive—not four basic types.

If a lawmaker lacks one or both of the restrictive attitudes
towards a given act, the resultant permissive attitudes can be
expressed in permissive laws. The two basic types of permissive
law parallel the two types of restriction. A non-command expresses the mere lack of a wish to see a given act performed,
the absence, that is, of the restrictive attitude that would be
expressed by commanding the same act. This permissive attitude should not be confused with a wish to see the act not performed: although not wanting to see the act performed is
compatible with a desire to see it not performed, the former
does not imply the latter. It follows that one can lack both
restrictive attitudes towards a given act and be content to see
it done or not done, or be content not to interfere. A non-
command is not the same as a prohibition. A non-prohibition
can be understood analogously: it expresses the absence of a
wish to see the act not performed without implying the wish
to see the act performed. Bentham offers these illustrations:

'Every householder shall carry arms': this is an example of a command: 'No householder shall carry arms': this of a prohibition:
'Any householder may forbear to carry arms': this, of a non-
command: 'Any householder may carry arms': this of a non-prohibition. (*OLG*, X, ii, 3)

In sum, Bentham maintains that four elementary legislative
attitudes must be distinguished, each of which can be expressed in a kind of law. There are therefore four basic types
of law, not merely restrictive commands and prohibitions.

---

[7] This point is of some interest, for it parallels conversion between predicative
statements such as the so-called *A* form statement and the corresponding *E*
form statement, discussed below.

Finally, law is not essentially imperatival but imperational.

Before looking more closely at the ways in which these types of law are supposed to be logically related, I should note one complication that the preceding summary has thus far ignored. In developing his full theory, Bentham varies his formulations, saying for example that a law or mandate 'expresses', 'manifests', or 'declares' the 'will', 'wish', or 'intention' of the 'sovereign', 'legislator', or 'magistrate'. Most of these variations need not detain us, but one is especially relevant to our concerns. Although Bentham often states that the attitude expressed by a restrictive imperation is a mere desire to see the act performed or not performed, sometimes he also refers to the lawmaker's wish 'to influence the conduct of the party in question' (*OLG*, X, ii, 2). This suggests that a restrictive law involves the sovereign's positive intention to interfere with and influence behaviour, a suggestion which accords with Bentham's frequent references to the sovereign's 'will' or 'volition' and with his definition of a law. Now Bentham is not likely to confuse the mere desire or wish to see an act performed with the positive intention to interfere and influence behaviour, if only because differences between them are related to his evaluation of acts and laws. He would distinguish between, say, wishing to see a certain act performed (because various interests would be served by it) and wishing to motivate the agent to perform it (which might not be worthwhile from an overall utilitarian standpoint, if the benefits that could be gained from the act would not exceed the costs of interference). A utilitarian legislator could register the former preference without acting on it, because he would always take into account the mischief produced by the law itself.

I suggest that the difference between these two kinds of attitude corresponds to the difference between imperations in general, which anyone can utter, and laws in particular, which are ascribable to the sovereign of a state. The logic of laws is a special case of the more general logic of imperations. Bentham develops his theory of imperations in terms of the law because it is his immediate concern; but he clearly wants it to apply outside that domain.[8] His theory concerns the logic

[8] In conjunction with Bentham's logic of imperation in *Laws*, one should also see *Introduction*, I, 2, note b; I, 14–II, 14; XVII, 29, note b2.

of what are now called 'normative' or 'prescriptive' utterances, including their permissive counterparts, outside as well as within the law. In fact, Bentham's approach implies the possibility of such parallels. His idea seems to be that we can understand the essential nature of laws by means of a simple model, based on some familiar relations between ordinary persons and the relevant sort of utterance that may pass between them. His use of the sovereign illustrates this point. Bentham does not imagine that the supreme lawmaking power in a political community must reside in a single individual, so the personification of this power in an individual 'sovereign' suggests an attempt to make down-to-earth sense, by analogy, of the extremely complicated, impersonal, and formal workings of the law.

The significance of the differences in formulations may then be this. The weaker attitude, the mere wish or desire, is the minimum expressed by any prescriptive imperational utterance, while the stronger attitude, that is, the intention of influencing behaviour, may be expressed only by a restrictive law. Any statement about, say, what ought to be done, can be taken as expressing the speaker's desire to see the act performed even if he is unwilling or unable to influence the conduct in question, while the sovereign by contrast does not merely say what ought to be done, but by his very nature endeavours to motivate compliance and is generally obeyed.

This distinction is also related to the difference, insisted upon by Bentham, between statements of what 'ought' to be done, which may only express the speaker's 'sentiments', and statements ascribing to individuals 'duties' or 'obligations' in the strictest sense. The latter, he thinks, imply the existence of sanctions to motivate their performance.[9] This distinction is an important weapon for Bentham in his battle against natural law, for he claims that natural lawyers, confusing what one ought to do with what one is under an obligation to do, mistakenly assume that their moral principles are embedded in the law.

---

9 *Introduction*, XVI, 25, note e2; *Fragment on Government*, ch. V, pars. 6–10; in Bowring, I, 292–4.

4. *The Logic of Imperation*

In his *Introduction* Bentham hints at a new logic, 'untouched by Aristotle', which concerns the principles of 'imperation' rather than 'argumentation' and deals with expressions of the speaker's 'will', not of his 'understanding' (*IPML*, XVII, 29, note e2). This is evidently the system he developed in *Of Laws in General*. Bentham's logical claims are not unambiguous, but for our purposes many theoretical complications can be ignored or touched on only briefly.

Among the four basic types of imperation, the possible relations respecting a given act are analogous to the relations held to exist among the four elementary types of subject-predicate propositions in traditional Aristotelian logic. The latter include the *A* form: 'All *S* is *P*' (for example, 'All swans are white'); the *E* form: 'No *S* is *P*' (for example, 'No swans are white'); the *I* form: 'Some *S* is *P*' (for example, 'Some swans are white'); and the *O* form: 'Some *S* is not *P*' (for example, 'Some swans are not white'). The four basic forms of imperation are somewhat problematic. Bentham's examples show that he does not require imperations in the law to be found in imperative form. But the examples concern classes of acts and individuals rather than single acts as performed by particular persons. Laws are typically of universal form, of course, but Bentham's logical claims are most straightforward and defensible when applied to very specific imperations.[10]

We might take the paradigm form of command to be, 'Do *A*' (directed at some person *P*), and 'Do not do *A*' as the form of a prohibition. The specific direction of these imperations can be indicated, however, in the following forms. Command: '*P* is to do *A*'; prohibition: '*P* is not to do *A*'; non-command: '*P* need not do *A*'; non-prohibition: '*P* may do *A*'. The relations claimed by Bentham among these four forms directly parallel the relations assumed to exist among propositional forms *A*, *E*, *I*, and *O*. We have already seen Bentham's principle of imperational conversion: just as 'All swans are white' can be regarded from a logical point of view as equivalent to 'No swans are not white', so 'Jones is to carry arms' is equi-

---

[10] We may suppose that universalized imperations can be constructed out of the specific ones.

valent to 'Jones is not to fail to carry arms'. Similar conversions
are possible between *I* and *O* forms and between corresponding non-commands and non-prohibitions. The rest of Bentham's new logic can be constructed around two principles,
which I shall call 'imperational contradiction' and 'imperational contrariety'. These principles are selected not because
Bentham makes either of them central but because the corresponding relations are familiar and fundamental in traditional logic and are crucial to any system like Bentham's.

The two main types of logical opposition in ordinary logic
are contradiction and contrariety; analogues to both are found
in Bentham's system. As it concerns complete statements, contradiction in ordinary logic is exemplified most plainly in the
relation between a statement and its denial. If one is true the
other is false, and if the one is false then the other is true;
they are said to have opposite 'truth values'. In the traditional
logic of predicative statements, such a relation obtains between corresponding *A* and *O* forms and between corresponding *E* and *I* forms (between 'All swans are white' and 'Some
swans are not white' on the one hand, and between 'No swans
are white' and 'Some swans are white' on the other). Contrariety, a weaker relation between statements, exists when
they cannot both be true though both might be false; from the
fact that one is true we can infer that the other is false, but
from one's being false we cannot conclude that the other is
true. In the traditional logic of predicative statements, *A* and
E forms are said to be contraries. 'All swans are white' and 'No
swans are white' are thus logically incompatible, but not contradictory, presuming that there are swans. In Bentham's
system, contradiction is paralleled by the chief relation claimed
to exist between restrictions and permissions, while contrariety is akin to the most important relation among restrictions themselves, that is, between commands and prohibitions
(cf. *OLG*, X, iv, 1).

Imperational Contradiction. In explaining permissive laws,
Bentham says that the non-command of a given act is the 'negation' of its command and that its non-prohibition is the 'negation' of its prohibition (*OLG*, X, ii, 3). Presumably he also
means that commands are negations of non-commands and
prohibitions negations of non-prohibitions, for the idea of

'being the negation of' something, as used in logic, is symmetrical. And his complete logic of imperation seems to require that the relation be symmetrical. Bentham may be taken as saying that 'Jones is to do A' and 'Jones may refrain from doing A' are in some sense contradictories, and that 'Jones is not to do A' and 'Jones may do A' are also contradictories. The prohibition and permission of the same act are supposed to be mutually exclusive and exhaustive of the possibilities. A self-consistent system of imperations would not include both, but it would contain one or the other. What all of this means is not entirely clear, but we can defer this problem for a moment.

Imperational Contrariety. Bentham contends that the command and prohibition of a given act 'are necessarily repugnant and exclusive' too, but he neither says, nor does he seem to mean, that one is the full-fledged negation of the other, since he allows that with no inconsistency an act might be neither commanded nor prohibited (OLG, X, ii, 7). The relation between 'Jones is to do A' and 'Jones is not to do A' therefore seems analogous to ordinary contrariety: they are incompatible but not contradictory. A self-consistent system of imperations would not include both the command and the prohibition of a given act, but it might include neither.

Given these two principles plus imperational conversion, we can reconstruct the whole of Bentham's logic of imperation. Two examples are especially important. In traditional logic, A forms and E forms are said to imply I forms and O forms respectively. For example, on the assumption that there are swans, 'All swans are white' implies 'Some swans are white'. This is called 'sub-alternation', and it has an analogue in Bentham's system. Thus the command of an act includes its permission, which can be shown by arguing that its command excludes its prohibition, which means that it includes the negation of a prohibition; this non-prohibition is a permission. Parallel reasoning shows that the prohibition of an act includes its non-command or, in other words, that its non-performance is permitted. In legal terms this means that one cannot possibly violate the law of a self-consistent system as long as one is either doing what it requires or abiding by its prohibitions.

We can also get the imperational analogue of sub-contrariety from our three principles. In its traditional form this means that corresponding I and O statements such as 'Some swans are white' and 'Some swans are not white' can both be true though they cannot both be false. In Bentham's system this becomes the claim that either an act or its non-performance must be permitted—possibly both, but at least one of them. Thus, for example, if an act is not permitted, then it must be prohibited; its non-performance is then commanded, and this implies that the non-performance is permitted. In legal terms this means that in a self-consistent system of law either an act or its non-performance must be lawful. At every behavioural junction it should be possible to act within the law.

Bentham thus describes with respect to a given act performed by an individual a complete, determinate set of logical relations among the four basic types of imperation, and specifically the four basic types of law. The results can be summarized by saying that an act can purportedly be dealt with in one, but only one, of three possible ways within a self-consistent system of imperations: (1) it may be commanded, (2) it may be prohibited, or (3) it may be left entirely free, neither commanded nor prohibited. There are no other possibilities, and these three cases completely determine the imperational condition of an act and its non-performance. These principles of imperational logic could be displayed on a 'square of opposition' such as the one often used for traditional logic.

5. The Interpretation of Bentham's New Logic

A few comments on Bentham's system are in order. One must ask, first, what Bentham means when he says that one imperation is the 'negation' of another. The problem is to understand how ordinary logical concepts can apply to imperations at all. They pre-eminently apply to and may be definable in terms of the relations between items such as statements that are supposed to be true or false. However, commands and prohibitions can be authorized or unauthorized, reasonable or unreasonable, and so on—but they cannot be described as true or false. When Bentham says that the command of an act is the negation of its non-command, we cannot take him to be saying that the command is *true* if and only if the non-command is *false*, for this has no apparent meaning. Similarly, since the command and prohibition of an act are not logical contraries in the ordinary sense, it is difficult to understand the claim that they are 'necessarily repugnant and exclusive'. Bentham's principles need an interpretation. He seems to be extending logical concepts so that they can be applied to items to which they ordinarily do not apply, but he does not explain the outcome.

It is important to emphasize that my concern here is with logical relations and nothing else. If a legal system, for example, contains conflicting statutes, so that officials are authorized to treat as criminal both doing something and refraining from it, then the system might be criticized as morally objectionable, as well as practically deficient. But these considerations have no direct bearing here. The question is, what is *logically* defective about conflicting laws? How should we understand the claim that two laws are 'inconsistent'?

The problem would be avoided if the items to which the principles of imperational logic apply were supposed to have 'truth values'. Bentham almost seems to avoid the difficulty in such a way, by suggesting that imperations are a specific kind of descriptive statement, unlike those dealt with by ordinary logic in that they express the speaker's volition and thus describe his will rather than express his beliefs and describe his understanding (*IPML*, XVII, 29, note b2). If Bentham thought this, then he presumably held that imperations are true or false. It would then be understandable for him to omit an account of imperational logic, for it would be no more than a sector or application of ordinary logic. But this interpretation is open to question. Bentham's discussion of the point is brief and confused and probably reflects a struggle to grasp the elusive distinction between asserting and expressing.[11] Bentham clearly wanted his logic to apply to laws and they are neither true nor false. If laws are imperations, then imperations are not a species of descriptive statement and their logic is not just a sector of ordinary logic. Bentham's logic still needs interpretation.

[11] It is possible to appreciate Bentham's difficulty if we note that the ambiguity of Hume's theory of moral language resulted in part from his failure to employ such a distinction. Hume never made clear whether he meant that moral judgements merely express one's attitudes or that they assert the existence of such attitudes. See, e.g., his *Treatise of Human Nature*, bk. III, pt. I, and *Enquiry Concerning the Principles of Morals*, sec. 1 and Appendix I.

It is natural to refer to imperationally contrary and contradictory laws as 'conflicting'. But what exactly does this mean? The nature of imperational contrariety seems clear: the same act is both required and forbidden, so it is impossible to satisfy the demands of both laws. One law must be broken. The nature of the conflict between imperationally contradictory laws, which require an act and permit its non-performance or forbid and permit a single act, is different, however. This is a conflict between permissive and restrictive laws. Since a permissive law makes no relevant demands on us, there are no permissive demands that can be inconsistent with those of any restrictions. A permissive law cannot be broken. The conflict here is analogous to the conflict between contradictory assertions: one takes back, so to speak, what the other gives. This account might be extended to cover imperational contrariety as well. If I order someone to do something and then, without rescinding the order, tell him he must not do it or he need not do it, I wind up in much the same incoherent position as if I had asserted something and then denied it without withdrawing my original assertion. The clearer I make it that I stand by both imperations, or both assertions, the more mysterious it becomes just what I could possibly mean. Bentham recognized that imperational discourse can be self-stultifying and thus that it has a 'logic'.

One might try to explain matters as follows. The existence of a law that forbids Jones to do A makes it the case that Jones is legally prohibited from doing A; the existence of a law allowing Jones to do A makes it the case that Jones is legally permitted to do A; and so on. But sentences of the form 'X is permitted' are contradictories of corresponding sentences of the form 'X is prohibited', by the meanings of 'permitted' and 'prohibited'. The trouble, then, with imperationally contradictory laws is that they would create contradictory states of affairs, which is logically impossible. If we assume that the command of an act includes its permission, then this account can be extended to cover imperational contrariety.

Such an approach minimizes the need to introduce new logical concepts and shows the extent to which imperational logic rests on ordinary logic even though it is not simply a sector or application of the latter. For there is no *formal* contradiction between imperations such as 'Jones is to do A' and 'Jones may refrain from doing A', or even between statements concerning imperations, such as 'Jones is required to do A' and 'Jones is permitted to refrain from doing A'. The conflict turns on the *substance* of what is said, that is, on the relations between such concepts as 'permitted', 'required', and 'forbidden'. Ordinary logical principles do not concern such specific matters.

This suggests that Bentham's principles should be understood as follows. Imperational contradiction requires that a restrictive law exists if and only if the corresponding permissive law does not exist. Imperational contrariety requires that conflicting commands and prohibitions do not co-exist. This means that any system of imperations, such as a system of law, must be self-consistent. There are no conflicting laws within legal systems.

Could Bentham have meant this? Statutes or judicial precedents do in fact sometimes conflict, but this interpretation of Bentham's logic precludes the very possibility of conflict. It seems to follow that either the interpretation is faulty or the logic is absurd. Of course, ordinary logic does not prevent the possibility of our making logical blunders. It does not describe our actual beliefs or discourse or guarantee that they will be consistent, but often serves as a critical standard for their coherence. Bentham's logic arguably should be viewed in a parallel way. He would not claim that a given act cannot be commanded and prohibited in a given system but only that such a system would be logically defective. It would not be impossible but flawed.

There is very strong evidence, however, that Bentham intended his logic to be understood in the former way. He so conceives of the 'sovereign's will' that restrictive and permissive legislative attitudes towards a given act are mutually exclusive and exhaustive of the possibilities; and he seems to hold that a law exists if and only if the sovereign has the corresponding legislative attitude (cf. *OLG*, X, ii, 8–9).

Although that approach rules out the possibility of conflicting laws, it is compatible with the sort of conflict under consideration. Bentham would not recognize conflicts between or within statutes and precedents as conflicts between *laws* in the theoretical complete sense of the term 'law' with which he is concerned. The need for such a theory, that is, the need at least for an interpretive notion of 'a law', can readily be seen. We do not simply read the laws or legal rules directly out of books, from which they emerge whole and in no further need of qualification. One must extract laws from legal documents and pronouncements, and sometimes they must be reconstructed out of dispersed items of law. What is contained in a single statute, judicial precedent, or administrative ruling is one thing, what is contained in a 'complete' law is quite another. Thus, one can have a notion of a 'law' which precludes the possibility of conflcting laws and yet concedes that particular documents and pronouncements actually conflict. If those conflicts cannot be resolved by ordinary legal criteria, then the law on the matter in question is so far indeterminate.

There is reason to believe that any system of deontic logic must be so understood when it is applied to the law, so Bentham's approach, on this interpretation, also appears to be sound.

7

MOTIVATION AND CONTROL

1. Abortive Solutions

To return to the main line of argument, we have seen that Bentham recognizes permissive as well as restrictive laws. In fact, he seems to regard them as logically on a par, for they are negations of each other. But he also maintains that there cannot be 'a law by which nobody is bound . . . by which nobody is coerced . . . by which nobody's liberty is curtailed'. This seems to preclude permissive laws which merely state what may or need not be done and do not bind, coerce, or curtail liberty.

One might try to dissolve the apparent contradiction as follows. Permissive laws indicate that certain persons have legal rights to behave in specified ways. But there are no personal rights without correlative obligations. One cannot have a right to do something unless others are prohibited from interfering. Permissive laws can therefore be said to bind, coerce, and curtail the liberty of those individuals whose interference they implicitly forbid. Thus, Bentham's recognition of permissive laws is compatible with the claim that all laws bind, coerce, and curtail liberty, and there is no real contradiction at all.

This argument fails, however, for several reasons. First, as we shall see, there is some basis for doubting that permissive laws *confer* legal liberties; they may simply confirm their existence. But if they do not confer such liberties, then it is questionable whether they can impose restrictions on interference. If we are speaking of laws that simply impose restrictions, then we are not speaking of permissive laws. Secondly, the alleged correlativity of rights and obligations is dubious. There is a straightforward sense of 'having a right' or 'being at liberty' to do something which entails no correlative obligations.[1] But we need not dispute the question now, for

[1] So I argue, at least, in 'The Correlativity of Rights and Duties', *Nous*, iv (1970), 45-55.

Bentham's theory alone is in question. He would not reason in the way suggested because he does not admit such correlations. He would allow that many rights imply correlative obligations, but he would not allow that the bare liberties included in permissive laws imply such obligations.[2] Bentham's notion of a permissive law amounts to the mere absence of a restrictive law, and this does not imply any corresponding restrictions.

It is possible, of course, to suggest some correlations to which he may be committed. For example, he might agree that to speak of *legal* liberty is to imply the context of a legal system, and he would probably hold that there cannot be a legal system unless there are some general restrictions on behaviour. From these assumptions it would follow that whenever someone is legally at liberty to do something, it is also true that others fall under restrictions. But this is irrelevant, for it does not show that permissive laws themselves bind, coerce, or curtail liberty. It shows only that such things happen concurrently with permissive laws. Bentham actually comes close to admitting the required correlations, for he holds that, as a matter of fact, interference with permitted behaviour is always prohibited. But he does not say that these prohibitions are implied by the permissive laws themselves; he says that they are always added (*OLG*, X, vi). And it is clear that his notion of a permissive law allows him no alternative. Restriction on anyone's behaviour requires a restrictive law. Bentham's permissive laws in themselves cannot be regarded as binding, coercing, or curtailing liberty, so his apparent contradiction still needs to be explained.

Another approach is suggested by Bentham's notion that 'every efficient law whatever may be considered as a limitation or exception, grafted on a pre-established law of liberty' (*OLG*, X, iv, 6). A legal system is thus conceived as restrictions imposed on a field of antecedently free behaviour. This image is powerfully drawn, in Bentham's most eloquent prose, more than once in *Of Laws in General* (cf. *OLG*, Appendix B, I, 3).

---

[2] Sometimes Bentham suggests that a right to do something implies a correlative obligation, and sometimes he suggests the opposite. See, e.g., Bowring, III, 159–60, 181, 217–18. The former view is compatible with the one attributed to him in the text, on the assumption that there is a relevant distinction between a 'right' and a bare 'permission'.

Why does he look at law in this way? As permissive laws are the 'negations' of restrictions, and vice versa, we might expect him to accept the opposite view just as readily, and be prepared to think of permissive laws imposed on a field of antecedently restricted behaviour. But he does not do so.

One explanation might be based on a formal or structural asymmetry within legal systems exemplified by the fact that a self-consistent system can subject an act to both kinds of permission but to only one kind of restriction. It could be argued that permissive laws are strictly superfluous while restrictive laws are not. There may be permissive as well as restrictive laws in ordinary legal systems, but for any given legal system can be imagined an equivalent one with no permissive laws at all, in which all the specific laws are restrictive— a *restrictive law* system. But we cannot coherently imagine an equivalent system with permissive but no restrictive laws, that is, a *permissive law* system. Permissive laws are thus eliminable in principle, while restrictive laws are not, so that a legal system can be regarded as essentially restrictive.

There is no doubt that Bentham leans in this direction. Consider the functions that he assigns to permissive laws (*OLG*, X, ii, 10; X, iv). They can be used to revoke restrictive laws and thus to restore liberties, to qualify or limit existing restrictions, and to clarify existing law in order, say, to allay unfounded fears about curtailed liberties. Two things are striking about this list of functions. First, it suggests that permissive laws do not confer liberties except by *restoring* them when they are used to qualify or revoke antecedently established restrictive laws. Second, these functions presuppose a system constructed around restrictions on behaviour. Permissive laws seem to have a secondary or parasitic role. Moreover, it may be possible to dispense with them entirely. Laws used to *confirm* the existence of legal liberties do not seem essential to a legal system. Laws used to qualify or limit restrictions might be eliminated too. One can at least imagine the alternative practice of revoking the laws that are to be qualified or limited and enacting suitably modified restrictive laws in their places. Indeed, it is unclear whether permissive laws that are used to qualify or limit restrictions should be regarded as independent, complete laws at all. They may constitute distinct enactments or judicial rulings, but once established they might best be regarded as elements of the restrictive laws that they qualify or limit. In any case, they seem theoretically eliminable.

This leaves the use of permissive laws to revoke restrictions entirely. If such changes are to be made, some laws of this general description would seem needed, and if provision for making such changes is essential to a sophisticated legal system, then permissive laws as a general class would not seem superfluous. But such laws would perform a very limited function within a legal system. Once they do their job of restoring liberties, neither the revoked nor the revoking laws should be thought of as contained in the resulting system.[3] The revoked laws no longer existing, the revoking laws have served their purpose, for liberties have thereby been restored. The revoking laws are part of the history of the system, but they do not determine its continuing content. What all the laws of a given system, taken together, require and allow, forbid and permit, I shall call their imperational content. It seems reasonable to suppose that the imperational content of any system of law at a given time could in principle be reproduced in a restrictive law system. Permissive laws might be needed to effect changes, but they would not be needed for any other essential purpose.[4]

This way of viewing a legal system ignores, of course, the implications of Bentham's principle of imperational contradiction as we have interpreted it. For that principle provides in effect a permissive law for every item of behaviour not restricted under the system, and thus permissive laws would not be eliminable. The only 'system' in which there would be no permissive laws is one completely devoid of lawful be-

---

[3] cf. Joseph Raz, *The Concept of a Legal System* (Clarendon Press, Oxford, 1970), pp. 58f., 76f.

[4] Bentham strongly implies such a view in *Laws*, XIV, 18. (I am indebted to H. L. A. Hart for indicating the significance of this passage to me.) In his important discussion of the individuality of a law in this chapter, Bentham seems to conceive of a system of law as purely restrictive. Here, as elsewhere, he so limits his discussion of permissive laws to 'de-obligative' laws as to imply that all permissive laws are de-obligative. I shall not discuss his theory of individuation for laws further except to say that its implications, too, apparently conflict with those of his imperational logic.

haviour, in which one could not possibly do *anything* without breaking the law.[5] Although this doubtful and in any case absurd possibility can be ignored, I shall pursue the image a bit further to show the contrast that is suggested.

Imagine, then, a system in which all the specific laws are restrictive, imposed upon a field of antecedently free behaviour. In effect, we are imagining a system in which there is a permissive background principle which says that whatever is not prohibited by a specific law of the system is permitted. It may be argued that it would be impossible to have the opposite sort of system, that is, one in which permissive laws are imposed upon a field of antecedently restricted behaviour, summarized in the background principle that whatever is not permitted by a specific law of the system is prohibited. To make an ordinary item of behaviour lawful in that system we would need a law to that effect. But any single item of behaviour is describable in indefinitely many ways, so that to 'liberate' just one action we would need to enact an infinite number of permissive laws, which is logically impossible. Thus permissive and restrictive laws are not on a par. We can conceive of ordinary legal systems as if their imperational content were determined by restrictive laws alone, but we cannot reproduce them, even in our imaginations, in a permissive law system.

This reasoning seems to me unsound. Not only would it be possible to liberate ordinary acts in a permissive law system, but we could also conceive of permissive law systems without conflicting restrictions, systems in which it is always possible for a person to act within the law. The error in this reasoning is the assumption that there must be in such a system a separate permissive law for each distinguishable aspect of human action that is to be made lawful. This is not necessary; we can cut wide swaths through the tangle of restrictions. To see how this can be done, consider the permissive law which says that anyone may do anything that does not harm or endanger others unless to avoid equal or greater harm or endangerment. Laws

5 For if an act is commanded and not prohibited, then the act, in Bentham's view, is permitted, and there is permissive law in the system. If an act is prohibited and not commanded, then the omission is permitted and there is permissive law in that case too.

such as this would surely liberate a great deal of behaviour, and they could be limited or supplemented as desired.[6]

This argument suggests that purely formal considerations are not likely to account for the asymmetry between restrictions and permissions in a legal system. Bentham does not suggest an argument of this type to explain his belief in such asymmetry, and we have now seen that he cannot be regarded as logically committed to the conclusion by such a route.

So I return to the relative functions of permissive and restrictive laws. Consider the two extreme, ideal systems we have sketched—one containing only permissive laws and the other containing only restrictive laws—with their respective contrasting background principles. It might be argued that the chief function of restrictions could not be performed within a permissive law system: commands and prohibitions lay down guidelines for behaviour, and show the paths that must or must not be taken. Permissive laws, however, provide no guidelines; they simply indicate what is permitted and thus cannot be used to channel behaviour in determinate directions.

This claim too is unsound. For there will be both permissions and restrictions in each system, even though there will be only one type of law in each. It can be granted that the specific functions of permissive and restrictive laws are different; but they do not function in isolation. When we know what restrictions are laid down in the restrictive law system, the permissive background principle enables us to determine what may and need not be done. Paths of free behaviour can be tracked among restrictions. Similarly, when we know what is permitted by the laws of a permissive system, the restrictive background principle tells us what is still commanded or prohibited. Here the permissive laws directly indicate the paths of lawful behaviour.

2. The 'Force' of a Law

So far, I have considered law chiefly in its role as a guide to action by virtue of its indicating what is 'commanded', 'prohibited', or 'permitted'. But Bentham's full conception of the law does not simply label behaviour 'lawful' or 'unlawful'.

---

[6] This reasoning should also meet the objection suggested by G. H. von Wright, *Norm and Action* (Routledge & Kegan Paul, London, 1963), pp. 86–8.

Laws are not merely devices used for expressing the sovereign's preferences about his subjects' conduct; they also indicate his positive intention to influence their conduct. Bentham builds into his definition of a 'law' reference to what he calls its *'force'*, which concerns 'the *motives* it relies on for enabling it to produce the effect it aims at' (*OLG*, I, 1). There is an essential motivational aspect to the law, and this is responsible for the asymmetry between restrictions and permissions.

Bentham conceives of the law as a system of social control.[7] What is meant by social control is not direct manipulation by means of chains, walls, bars, drugs, or other such devices. These may be used by the law, but they do not fully explain the mode of control in question, which is getting people to behave in certain ways by affecting their own *self*-control through the use of rules and guidelines for them to follow. These rules neither move nor restrain the movement of persons, but they are understood to indicate what one is expected to do. How is control *effected* by means of such rules? Bentham's answer is that motivation must be supplied. In some cases pre-existing motivation can be exploited; but motivation is in any case relied upon.

Motivation accounts for the asymmetry between restrictions and permissions for it concerns restrictions in a way it could not possibly concern permissions. This does not mean that, as a matter of fact, legal sanctions are required to goad people into compliance with restrictive laws, while none is normally required to induce people to comply with permissive laws. It means, rather, that no sense can be attached to the idea of motivating someone to comply with, obey, conform to, or follow a permissive law, for permissive laws, which have no restrictive implications, cannot possibly be broken. But it makes a great deal of sense to speak of motivating someone to abide by a restriction, for he might otherwise fail to do so. What Bentham thought of as the essential element of motivation in the law would seem, therefore, to have special significance for restrictions. Even though there can be permissive laws, commands and prohibitions do the work of guiding behaviour. Control is exercised through such laws, with per-

---

[7] If the law has other functions, they are, in Bentham's view, reducible to or derivable from this primary one.

missions providing only the needed contrast. This is why Bentham calls such laws 'efficient'. And this is why he conceives of the law *as if* it were a system of restrictions.

I do not mean that restrictive laws are always efficacious. Bentham surely would not insist on that, especially in a system that does not satisfy the dictates of utility. Nor do I mean that permissive laws can never be used to channel behaviour. By drawing attention to lawful forms of behaviour, by creating desires, and so on, an enactment which simply confirms the existence of certain permissions may lead people to take advantage of them. Bentham would indeed be happy to use the comparatively mischiefless device of permissive laws for such a purpose; but he clearly doubts that they would often be efficacious. He contends that motivation and control are exercised through restrictive laws. This contention could not be maintained as a logically necessary truth, however. The asymmetry of restrictive and permissive laws thus rests to some degree on logically contingent factors.

But there is another aspect of Bentham's concept of the law as essentially restrictive. He accepts a Hobbesian picture of political society.[8] Hobbes defines a 'state of nature' as a condition without enforced restrictive rules, and this is how Bentham understands the term. In such a state there are innumerable 'natural rights' because there are no enforced restrictions. In making law we introduce restrictions, imposing them upon the antecedent field of natural rights or liberties, thereby extinguishing some of them. Their residue remains within the political system, where they are called 'political' or 'legal' liberties. Political liberty is thus seen as continuous with or as a species of natural liberty—a subtle manifestation of the philosophical 'naturalism' of both Hobbes and Bentham. To make law is to *add* something to the world. What is added cannot be liberty, for that was there already. Law adds restrictions or obligations and thus takes away previously existing liberty. Hobbes reasons this way because he regards enforced restrictions as 'impediments' to action: the threat of sanctions serves to avert one from certain actions.[9] Bentham shares this view. It is part of Bentham's very concept of what it is for there

---

[8] See *Leviathan*, e.g., chs. XIII–XIV, XVII, XXI, XXVI, to reconstruct this view.   [9] *Leviathan*, ch. XXI.

to *be* a legal system. The roots of his idea that restrictive laws are the efficient or really operative ones thus go very deep; they are anchored in his nominalist and empiricist metaphysics.

When Bentham says that all laws bind, coerce, and curtail liberty, he means not that there cannot be permissive laws, but that the law as a whole can be viewed *as if* there were none. Permissive laws may be used to restore liberties, but they are not needed for describing the imperational content of a system at any time. It may be granted that the principle of imperational contradiction requires permissive laws for any unrestricted behaviour. Bentham collects this indefinitely large class of permissive laws under one permissive background principle which says that whatever is not prohibited by a specific law of the system is permitted. But he refuses to view the law in the alternative way, as permissions imposed on a field of restrictions, because his way seems to correspond with two important aspects of reality. First, restrictive laws are supposed to be the instruments of behavioural control. Second, the permissive background principle indicates that political liberty is conceived of as a species of natural liberty. Law gives us direction and control exercised through a central power or sovereign. It adds restrictions to the world. It adds no permissions—or liberty—at all.

3. *The Need for Coercive Sanctions*

Bentham's claim that all laws are necessarily coercive can be understood as referring *only* to 'efficient' laws, or restrictions. Can we now conclude that Bentham regarded *these* laws, at least, as invariably and essentially coercive? His actual position is not quite so simple.

Bentham says, in effect, that subjects must generally be motivated to obey their sovereign's restrictive laws; this follows from his notions of a law and of a sovereign. But this is not to say that restrictive laws are coercive, which would suggest that the motivation in question must be provided by the threat of legal punishment. There is another gap in Bentham's position, between the claim that efficient (restrictive) laws are necessarily coercive and the mere condition that conformity generally be motivated. How is this gap to be bridged?

First of all, when Bentham speaks of 'sanctions', he means no more than a source of motivation (*OLG*, VI, 19; XI, 2; cf. *IPML*, III). 'Coercive' sanctions motivate by the prospect of pain or some other unpleasant or unwanted condition. There are also 'alluring' sanctions which attract rather than repel, by the prospect of pleasure instead of pain (*OLG*, XI, 2). Bentham's references to 'coercion' might therefore be to some extent misleading. They do not necessarily refer to punishment or in fact to any legally authorized sanctions; they only imply that the psychological mechanism is aversion. Moreover, the idea of punishment is not implicit in Bentham's notion of a law, for he allows the possibility of using rewards instead of coercive sanctions. He urges, however, that they be used only for supplementary motivation because punishments are more effective, reliable, and predictable, and thus generally more useful (*OLG*, XI, 6–9). Finally, although Bentham requires that laws generally be obeyed, he does not hold that law itself must always provide the necessary motivation. General conformity is sometimes a consequence of a mere 'habit' of obedience or a 'disposition' on the part of subjects to comply with the law (*OLG*, X, III, 8). In specific cases, Bentham recognizes that sanctions may be supplied by religion or conventional morality (*OLG*, VI, 19; cf. Appendix A, 4).

In sum, it is only on contingent grounds that Bentham shows a close connection between legally authorized coercive sanctions and individual laws, and then only on the assumption of a rational or utilitarian legislator. Bentham believes that, as a matter of fact, sanctions are generally coercive and legally authorized, and this is the way any rationally constructed system of law would have it. Only in that respect, then, would Bentham seem committed to the idea that restrictions, and thus 'all laws', are *essentially* coercive.

To this degree, therefore, his claim that all laws are coercive and consequently mischievous cannot be reconciled with his fully elaborated legal philosophy. This claim is either a vestige of his early crude theorizing about the law or else it is an oversimplification. If the law can be viewed as a restrictive system, then Bentham may be entitled to say that all laws, meaning all efficient laws, are restrictive. Restrictive laws are of the type to which coercive sanctions can be attached. But they are not *necessarily* coercive.

We are now in a position to see why the relation between law and obligation is also problematic in Bentham.[10] He often speaks as if laws were essentially obligative, but this does not reflect his fully elaborated theory of law. Like Hobbes and Hume before him, Bentham sometimes suggests that obligations are simply acts that one is somewhat motivated to perform.[11] All that is needed is a 'sanction', or a source of motivation. However, this leads to rather implausible 'obligations', including those that would result from the 'physical sanction' alone, which is the natural sequence of cause and hedonic effect. On this view, if some activity is unpleasant, one would be 'under an obligation' to avoid it. More often, however, Bentham suggests that the stronger and consequently more plausible condition for being under an obligation is that there be a restriction to which punishment is attached as a sanction for non-compliance. But if restrictive laws are not necessarily coercive, then on this view neither are they necessarily obligative. The logical gap we have seen between law and coercion in Bentham's theory also creates a gap between law and obligation.

I have just noted the possibility of restrictive laws backed only by 'alluring' sanctions or inducements. This notion presumes that rewards or other inducements are offered as a way of getting people to do certain things. But notice how different such laws would be from ordinary restrictions. Commands or prohibitions backed by sanctions would be understood to say, in effect, that certain behaviour is lawful and other behaviour unlawful. But suppose we have restrictions backed only by inducements. These look more like invitations. And one failing to take advantage of an offered inducement does not thereby act unlawfully. It would seem, however, that this distinction

10 See *Introduction*, III, 2, note a; XVI, 25, note e2; *Fragment on Government*, ch. V, pars. 6–7, notes; in Bowring, I, 292–4.

11 A conjunction of ch. XIV and XXI of *Leviathan* can suggest that this was Hobbes's view of what an obligation *is*; and Hume also suggests some such thing in his *Treatise of Human Nature*, bk. III, pt. II, sec. 1. In neither case, however, would this perhaps be the best rendering of their most considered ideas about obligation.

is relatively unimportant to Bentham since he assimilates such laws to restrictions backed by coercive sanctions.

Bentham views them in this way because he believes that the mechanism exploited by adding motivation is essentially the same in either case: the sovereign makes one type of action more attractive or less unattractive than another. It makes no difference in principle whether one is threatened with punishment for doing X or offered an inducement for not doing X. Either method makes the non-performance of X more attractive. The main difference between these alternative approaches is supposed to be their relative efficiencies. If this is a correct understanding of Bentham, it suggests how important the motivational and control elements are to his concept of the law. From other points of view one would not so readily assimilate restrictive laws supported by rewards to those supported by coercive sanctions.

Thus, Bentham's basic conception of law should not be characterized as an Austinian imperative theory. It is true that Austin shared Bentham's approach to understanding law and that their conclusions about the nature of a legal system were similar. But the details of their views are significantly different. Bentham recognized laws that are permissive and thus 'unimperative'. To some degree, this follows from his 'logic of imperation': if some behaviour is either not commanded or not prohibited then the principle of imperational contradiction entitles one to say that corresponding permissive laws exist. But permissive laws were not merely such logical constructs for Bentham. He also held that actual enactments could sometimes be understood in whole or in part as permissive laws. Such laws may occupy a secondary place within a legal system, but they nevertheless do exist.

Permissive laws are necessarily uncoercive and unobligative, for on Bentham's analysis they are *purely* permissive and not at all restrictive. But even Bentham's restrictive or 'imperative' laws are not necessarily coercive or obligative. Bentham was unclear about the relations between sanctions and the restrictions they are supposed to support, but he did indicate that laws used only to lay down guidelines for behaviour can be neither coercive nor obligative. Some laws might rely on extra-legal sanctions entirely, and rewards might be used instead of punishments to motivate behaviour. Bentham allowed these things to be possible, but he maintained that they would not be wise: he thought that rewards and extra-legal sanctions were so unreliable that any guidelines worth propounding *ought* to be supported firmly by legally authorized coercive sanctions. Here Bentham doffs his analytical cap, dons his utilitarian helmet, and maintains in effect that all 'efficient' laws—all laws for directing behaviour—are *essentially* coercive. But this is more a recommendation than a discovery.

BIBLIOGRAPHY

I. WORKS BY OR ASCRIBED TO BENTHAM

A. MAJOR COLLECTIONS IN ENGLISH

The Works of Jeremy Bentham, published under the superintendence of his literary executor, John Bowring. 11 vols. Wm. Tait, Edinburgh, 1838–43 (reissued Russell & Russell, N.Y., 1962).

Although it is being superseded by the new *Collected Works* (below), the Bowring edition is currently the main source of published Bentham material. It is incomplete (e.g., books have since been unearthed in Bentham's MSS., and Bowring excluded anticlerical materials) and unreliable (e.g., many items in it were constructed from MSS., sometimes supplemented with published materials, which are not always from Bentham's hand).

GUIDE TO THE BOWRING EDITION. No such guide seems otherwise available, even in the edition itself. It indicates most of Bentham's publications during his lifetime (dates are of the first appearance of previously published works, according to the best available information).

Volume I

General Preface, by W.W., v–xv.

List of Errata, 1–2.

Introduction to the Study of the Works of Jeremy Bentham, by John Hill Burton, 3–83.

An Introduction to the Principles of Morals and Legislation, 1789, i–xiii, 1–154. (Text from 1823 edn., with insertions from Dumont's *Traités*; see sect. I.B, below.)

Essay on the Promulgation of Laws, 155–68. (Based on MSS. and printed works.)

Essay on the Influence of Time and Place in Matters of Legislation, 169–94. (Based on MSS.)
A Table of the Springs of Action, 1817, 195–219.
A Fragment on Government 1776, 221–95. (Text from 1823 edn., with added Historical Preface.)
Principles of the Civil Code, 297–364. (Based on Dumont's *Traités* and MSS., with Appendix, Of the Levelling System.)
Principles of Penal Law, 365–580. (Based on Dumont's *Traités* and *Théorie* and MSS., here with Appendix, On Death-Punishment, published 1831.)

Volume II
Principles of Judicial Procedure, 1–188. (Based on MSS.)
The Rationale of Reward, 1825, 189–266. (Based on Dumont's *Théorie*, here with added Appendix.)
Leading Principles of a Constitutional Code, 1823, 267–74.
On the Liberty of the Press, and Public Instruction, 1821, 275–97.
An Essay on Political Tactics, 299–373. (Based on Dumont's *Tactique* and MSS., fragment published 1791.)
The Book of Fallacies, 1824, 375–487.
Anarchical Fallacies, 489–534. (Originally in Dumont's *Tactique*.)
Principles of International Law, 535–60. (Based on MSS., here with Appendix, Junctiana Proposal.)
A Protest Against Law-Taxes, 1795, 573–83.
Supply without Burden, 1795, 585–98.
Tax with Monopoly, 599–600.

Volume III
Defense of Usury, 1787, 1–29.
A Manual of Political Economy, 31–84. (Based on Dumont's *Théorie* and MSS.)
Observations on the Restrictive and Prohibitory Commercial System, 1821, 85–103.
A Plan ... [Circulating Annuities, &c.], 105–53. (Based on MSS.)
A General View of a Complete Code of Laws, 155–210. (Based on MSS. and various printed works.)
Pannomial Fragments, 211–30. (Based on MSS.)
Nomography, 231–95. (Based on MSS., here with Appendix, Logical Arrangements.)
Equity Dispatch Court Proposal, 1830, 297–317.
Equity Dispatch Court Bill, 319–431. (Based on MSS.)
Plan of Parliamentary Reform, 1818, 433–557.
Radical Reform Bill, 1819, 558–97.
Radicalism not Dangerous, 599–622. (Based on MSS.)

Volume IV

A View of the Hard-Labour Bill, 1778, 3–35.
Panopticon: or the Inspection-House, 1791, 37–172. (Published with Postscripts published 1791 and Note.)
Panopticon *versus* New South Wales, 1802, 173–248.
A Plea for the Constitution, 1803, 249–84.
Draught of a Code for the Organization of Judicial Establishment in France, 1790, 285–304.
Bentham's Draught ... compared with that of the National Assembly, 1790, 305–406.
Emancipate Your Colonies!, 1830, 407–18.
Jeremy Bentham to his Fellow-Citizens of France, 1830, 419–50.
Papers Relative to Codification and Public Instruction, 1817, 451–533.
Codification Proposal, 1822, 535–94.

Volume V

Scotch Reform, 1808, 1–53 + Tables.
Summary View of the Plan of a Judicatory, 1808, 55–60.
The Elements of the Art of Packing, 1821, 61–186.
'Swear Not At All', 1817, 187–229.
Truth *versus* Ashurst, 1823, 231–37.
The King *against* Edmonds, 1820, 239–51.
The King *against* Sir Charles Wolseley, 1820, 253–61.
Official Aptitude Maximised; Expense Minimised, 1830, 263–386.
A Commentary on Mr. Humphrey's Real Property Code, 1826, 387–416.
Outline of a Plan of a General Register of Real Property, 1832, 417–35.
Justice and Codification Petitions, 1829, 437–548.
Lord Brougham Displayed, 549–612. (Parts published 1831–2.)

Volume VI

Introductory View of the Rationale of Evidence, printed 1812, 1–187
Rationale of Judicial Evidence, 1827, 189–585. (Text continued in Vol. VII.)

Volume VII

Rationale of Judicial Evidence (continued), 1–600.
General Index to Vols. VI–VII, 601–44.

Volume VIII
Chrestomathia, 1816–17, 1–191.
Fragment on Ontology, 192–211. (Based on MSS.)
Essay on Logic, 213–93. (Based on MSS.)
Essay on Language, 294–338. (Based on MSS.)
Fragments on Universal Grammar, 339–57. (Based on MSS.)
Tracts on Poor Laws and Pauper Management, 1797, 358–439.
Observations on the Poor Bill, 1797, 440–61.
Three Tracts Relative to Spanish and Portuguese Affairs, 1821, 463–86.
Letters to Count Toreno, on the Proposed Penal Code, 1822, 487–554.
Securities Against Misrule, Adapted to a Mahommedan State, 555–600. (Based on MSS.)

Volume IX
Constitutional Code, v–x, 1–662. (Parts published 1830–1.)

Volume X
Memoirs and Correspondence, 1–606. (Continued in Vol. XI.)

Volume XI
Index to Memoirs and Correspondence, i–iv.
Memoirs and Correspondence (continued), 1–170.
Analytical Index to the Works, i–cccxci.

The Collected Works of Jeremy Bentham, general editor J. H. Burns. (Expected to include about 38 vols.) Athlone Press, London, 1968– .
   This promises to be comprehensive and definitive and has made a good start. Volumes already published are:

Correspondence. Vol. I (1752–76), ed. T.L.S.Sprigge, 1968. Vol. II (1777–80), ed. T.L.S.Sprigge, 1968. Vol. III (1781–8), ed. Ian R.Christie, 1971. (The editors' Introductions provide accurate information on Bentham's life.)
An Introduction to the Principles of Morals and Legislation, ed. J.H.Burns and H.L.A.Hart, 1970.
Of Laws in General, ed. H.L.A.Hart, 1970. (A new edn. of the book first published as *The Limits of Jurisprudence Defined*; see sect. I.c, below.)

B. SOME WORKS FIRST PUBLISHED IN FRENCH

These are based on MSS. supplied by Bentham as well as published works, but come directly from the hand of Étienne Dumont.

Traités de législation civile et pénale. 3 vols. Paris, 1802. (First English translation, by Neal, Boston, 1830; first English edn. in U.K., by Hildreth, 1864, as *The Theory of Legislation*, which is thus twice removed from Bentham. Portions included in Bowring edn. of *Works*, Vol. I.)

Théorie des peines et des récompenses. 2 vols. London, 1811. (Translated by Smith as *The Rationale of Reward*, 1825, and *The Rationale of Punishment*, 1830. Portions in Bowring edn. of *Works*, Vols. I–III.)

Tactique des assemblées législatives, suivie d'un traité des sophismes politique, 2 vols. Geneva, 1816. (A fragment published 1791 as *Essay on Political Tactics*; at least part published 1824 as *The Book of Fallacies*, ed. Bingham. Portions in Bowring edn. of *Works*, Vol. II.)

Traité des preuves judiciares. 2 vols. Paris, 1823. (English version, *A Treatise on Judicial Evidence*, by Dumont, 1825.)

C. SOME PUBLICATIONS NOT IN THE BOWRING EDITION

Deontology; or the Science of Morality, ed. Bowring. 2 vols. Wm. Tait, London and Edinburgh, 1834.

A Comment on the Commentaries, ed. C.W.Everett. Clarendon Press, Oxford, 1928. (Based on MSS. of 1775, this is the rest of the work from which *A Fragment on Government* was torn.)

The Limits of Jurisprudence Defined, ed. C.W.Everett. Columbia University Press, N.Y., 1945. (Based on MSS. discovered by Everett, this edn. is now superseded by *Of Laws in General* in the new *Collected Works*; see sect. I.A, above.)

D. OTHER, RECENT EDITIONS OF SOME WORKS

A Bentham Reader, ed. Mary P.Mack. Pegasus, N.Y., 1969.

A Fragment on Government & An Introduction to the Principles of Morals and Legislation, ed. Wilfrid Harrison. Blackwell, Oxford, 1960.

An Introduction to the Principles of Morals and Legislation, ed. Laurence J.Lafleur. Hafner, N.Y., 1948.

Bentham's Handbook of Political Fallacies, ed. Harold A.Larrabee. Harper, N.Y., 1962.

Bentham's Theory of Fictions, ed. C.K.Ogden. Littlefield, Adams, Paterson, N.J., 1959. (Ogden provides a long, informative introduction. A very useful compilation.)
Jeremy Bentham, ed. C.W.Everett. Dell, N.Y., 1966. (Half selections, half Everett's introduction.)
Jeremy Bentham's Economic Writings, ed. W.Stark. 3 vols. Allen & Unwin, London, 1952–4. (Based on both MSS. and published materials.)
The Theory of Legislation, ed. C.K.Ogden. Harcourt, Brace, N.Y., 1931. (With a long, informative introduction.)

II. SOME WORKS ON BENTHAM

This is a brief list of works with some special reference to Bentham. General discussions of relevant philosophical issues and further bibliographies on them can most conveniently be found in the *Encyclopedia of Philosophy*, ed. Paul Edwards (Macmillan & Free Press, N.Y., 1967), 8 vols.

BAUMGARDT, DAVID, *Bentham and the Ethics of Today* (Princeton University Press, 1952).
BRANDT, RICHARD B., *Ethical Theory* (Prentice-Hall, Englewood Cliffs, N.J., 1959).
D'ARCY, ERIC, *Human Acts* (Oxford, 1963).
EVERETT, CHARLES WARREN, *The Education of Jeremy Bentham* (Columbia University Press, N.Y., 1931).
GOLDWORTH, AMNON, 'The Meaning of Bentham's Greatest Happiness Principle', *Journal of the History of Philosophy*, vii (1969), 315–21.
HALÉVY, ELIE, *The Growth of Philosophic Radicalism*, tr. Mary Morris (Faber and Faber, London, 1928). (A valuable bibliography on Bentham compiled by C.W.Everett is appended to this edn.)
HALL, EVERETT W., 'The Proof of Utility in Bentham and Mill', *Ethics*, lx (1949), 1–18.
HART, H.L.A., 'Beccaria and Bentham', *Atti del Convegno su Chesare Beccaria* (Turin, 1966).
—— 'Bentham', *Proceedings of the British Academy*, xlviii (1962), 297–320.
—— 'Bentham on Legal Powers', *Yale Law Journal*, lxxxi (1972), 799–822.
—— 'Bentham on Legal Rights', forthcoming in *Oxford Essays in Jurisprudence, Second Series*.

—— 'Bentham on Sovereignty', *The Irish Jurist*, ii (N. S., 1967), 327–35.

—— 'Bentham's "Of Laws in General" ', *Rechtstheorie*, ii (1971), 55–66.

—— *Definition and Theory in Jurisprudence*. Inaugural Lecture, (Clarendon Press, Oxford, 1953). Reprinted in *Law Quarterly Review*, lxx (1954).

—— 'Positivism and the Separation of Law and Morals', *Harvard Law Review*, lxxi (1958), 593–629.

—— *Punishment and Responsibility* (Clarendon Press, Oxford, 1968).

—— *The Concept of Law* (Clarendon Press, Oxford, 1961).

HIMMELFARB, GERTRUDE, 'The Haunted House of Jeremy Bentham', in *Victorian Minds* (Knopf, N.Y., 1968), pp. 32–81.

KEETON, GEORGE W., and GEORG SCHWARZENBERGER, eds., *Jeremy Bentham and the Law: A Symposium* (Greenwood, Westport, Conn., 1970).

LYONS, DAVID, 'Logic and Coercion in Bentham's Theory of Law', *Cornell Law Review*, lvii (1972), 335–62.

—— 'On Sanctioning Excuses', *Journal of Philosophy*, lxvi (1969), 646–60.

—— 'Rights, Claimants, and Beneficiaries', *American Philosophical Quarterly*, vi (1969), 173–85.

—— 'Was Bentham a Utilitarian?', *Reason and Reality; Royal Institute of Philosophy Lectures* (Macmillan, London, 1972). pp. 196–221.

MACK, MARY PETER, *Jeremy Bentham: An Odyssey of Ideas* (Columbia University Press, N.Y., 1963).

MANNING, DAVID JOHN, *The Mind of Jeremy Bentham* (Longmans, London, 1968).

MILL, JOHN STUART, *Essays on Ethics, Religion and Society*, ed. J.M.Robson, *The Collected Works of John Stuart Mill*, Vol. X (University of Toronto Press, 1969. (This volume contains all of Mill's 'Bentham', 'Obituary of Bentham', 'Remarks on Bentham's Philosophy', and the 'Comment on Bentham' attributed to him.)

MILNE, A.TAYLOR, *Catalogue of the Manuscripts of Jeremy Bentham in the Library of University College London* (Athlone Press, London, 1962).

MONRO, D.H., 'Bentham'. In the *Encyclopedia of Philosophy*, ed. Paul Edwards (Macmillan & Free Press, N.Y., 1967), i, 280–5.

OGDEN, C.K., *Jeremy Bentham, 1832–2032* (Kegan Paul, London, 1932).

PINCOFFS, EDMUND, *The Rationale of Legal Punishment* (Humanities, N.Y., 1966).
PLAMENATZ, JOHN P., *The English Utilitarians.* Rev. edn. (Blackwell, Oxford, 1958).
Psyche, Vols. VIII–XVII (1928–37) contain many articles on Bentham.
SIDGWICK, HENRY, *Outlines of the History of Ethics for English Readers* (Macmillan, London, 1962).
STEPHEN, LESLIE, *History of English Thought in the Eighteenth Century*, 2 vols. (Harcourt, Brace & World, N.Y., 1963). Vol. II.
—— *The English Utilitarians.* 3 vols. (Kelley, Clifton, N.J., 1968). Vol. I.
VINER, JACOB, 'Bentham and J.S.Mill: The Utilitarian Background', *The Long View and the Short* (Free Press, Glencoe, Ill., 1958). 306–31.
WISDOM, JOHN, *Interpretation and Analysis in Relation to Bentham's Theory of Definition* (Kegan Paul, London, 1931).

INDEX

alluring sanction, 134f.
altruism, 65 (*see also* psychological egoism)
animals' interests, 19, 23, 26, 30
antipathy, 23, 66, 71, 73, 100
Aristotle, 117
art of:
  education, 96f.
  government, 30f., 82, 96 (*see also* public ethics)
  legislation, 33, 52–61, 72–4
  self-government, 30f., 56, 82f., 96 (*see also* private ethics)
Austin, J., 107f., 110f., 136

Beccaria, C., 3n, 8
beneficence required by utility, 19f., 23–34, 64, 73, 104f. (*see also* parochial interpretation)
Bentham, Samuel, 5
Blackstone, W., 7f.
Bowring, J., xiiif., 10f.
Burns, J. H., viii, xiiif., 11n

Chrestomathia, 45, 87, 96
Codification Proposal, 25n
coercion, 48, 108–16, 133–7
Collected Works of Jeremy Bentham, xiiif., 11
commands, vii, 107f., 112–14, 117–23, 130f., 135
Comment on the Commentaries, 7, 10f.
community interest standard, vii, 20, 24–34, 86, 101–3 (*see also* public ethics)
conflict and convergence of interests, 15f., 18, 24, 36, 38, 41–3, 45f., 54f., 58f., 62, 64f., 68f., 87f., 100
conflict of:
  laws, 121–4, 129
  principles, 35–43
Constitutional Code, 7, 25n, 66–9, 73, 87, 101f.
conventional morality, 56

conversion, logical, 113f., 117–19
contradiction, 118–23, 128, 133, 136
contrariety, 118–23
Copleston, F., 80n
correlativity of rights and obligations, 91, 125f.

Defense of Usury, 7
deontic logic, vii, 108, 112–24
Deontology, 10, 51n, 66
determinism, 14
deterrence, 57, 62, 72, 84
differential interpretation, vii, 20, 31–4, 52, 76–105
division of ethics, 29–34, 44f., 80, 82f., 95–9
dual standard, vii, 20–61, 64f., 73–100
Dumont, É., 10f., 51n
duty to oneself or others, 64, 73, 104f.

egoism:
  ethical, 13–15, 37, 39, 80
  psychological, 12–18, 63–74
  (*see also* hedonism)
empiricism, 90, 133
enforcement of morals, 58
Essay on Political Tactics, 25n
ethics: *see* division of ethics, private ethics, public ethics
Everett, C. W., xiv

fictions, linguistic, 75, 77f., 89–91
force of a law, 111, 131
Fragment on Government, 7f., 51–3n, 68, 99, 116n, 135n
functions of laws, 127f., 130–37

government:
  art of, 30f., 82, 96 (*see also* public ethics)
  personified, 31f., 77f., 85, 89–92, 94f., 116
  resistance to, 52n, 103f.

150 INDEX